The Mysterious & Unknown

Prophecies and Soothsayers

by Stuart A. Kallen

ReferencePoint Press®

San Diego, CA

About the Author
Stuart A. Kallen is a prolific author who has written more than 250 nonfiction books for children and young adults over the past 20 years. His books have covered countless aspects of human history, culture, and science, from the building of the pyramids to the music of the twenty-first century. Some of his recent titles include *Vampire Lore, Ancient Egypt,* and *Renewable Energy.* Kallen is also an accomplished singer-songwriter and guitarist in San Diego, California.

©2012 ReferencePoint Press, Inc.
Printed in the United States

For more information, contact:
ReferencePoint Press, Inc.
PO Box 27779
San Diego, CA 92198
www.ReferencePointPress.com

Picture credits:
Cover: Thinkstock/iStockphoto
© Alinari Archives/Corbis: 27
© Blue Lantern Studio/Corbis: 17
The Death of Julius Caesar, c.1446-50 (panel), Giovanni di Tommaso Angelo, (Giovagnolo) (d.1511)/Pushkin Museum, Moscow, Russia /The Bridgeman Art Library International: 11
© Corbis: 51
© Julie Dermansky/Corbis: 57
© JGSDF/Corbis: 7
© Lebrecht Music & Arts/Corbis: 44
© Roberto Rabanne/Sygma/Corbis: 39
Snark/Art Resource, NY: 61
© Stapleton Collection/Corbis: 33
Thinkstock/Digital Vision: 76
Thinkstock/Hemera: 69, 85

LIBRARY OF CONGRESS CATALOGING-IN-PUBLICATION DATA

Kallen, Stuart A., 1955-
  Prophecies and soothsayers / by Stuart A. Kallen.
     p. cm. -- (Mysterious & unknown)
  Includes bibliographical references and index.
  ISBN-13: 978-1-60152-184-2 (hardback)
  ISBN-10: 1-60152-184-7 (hardback)
  1. Prophecies (Occultism) 2. Bible--Prophecies. I. Title.
  BF1791.K35 2012
  133.3--dc22   2011006886

CONTENTS

FOREWORD

"Strange is our situation here upon earth."
—*Albert Einstein*

Since the beginning of recorded history, people have been perplexed, fascinated, and even terrified by events that defy explanation. While science has demystified many of these events, such as volcanic eruptions and lunar eclipses, some remain outside the scope of the provable. Do UFOs exist? Are people abducted by aliens? Can some people see into the future? These questions and many more continue to puzzle, intrigue, and confound despite the enormous advances of modern science and technology.

It is these questions, phenomena, and oddities that Reference-Point Press's *The Mysterious & Unknown* series is committed to exploring. Each volume examines historical and anecdotal evidence as well as the most recent theories surrounding the topic in debate. Fascinating primary source quotes from scientists, experts, and eyewitnesses as well as in-depth sidebars further inform the text. Full-color illustrations and photos add to each book's visual appeal. Finally, source notes, a bibliography, and a thorough index provide further reference and research support. Whether for research or the curious reader, *The Mysterious & Unknown* series is certain to satisfy those fascinated by the unexplained.

INTRODUCTION

Practicing the Art of Prophecy

Sometime around AD 1600, a book was published by an unnamed soothsayer. It contained a recipe for a magic potion that would allow users to see into the future and make prophecies: "Take of the [gallbladder] of a male Cat, and the fat of a Hen all white, and mix them together, and anoint thy eyes and thou shalt see it that others cannot see."[1] Such concoctions were typical in ancient times when soothsayers used all manner of animal parts to predict the future. As long ago as 2500 BC, soothsayers studied the shapes of sheep or chicken guts, seeking signs of calamity or good fortune. On particularly important occasions, soothsayers read the entrails of dead people.

Soothsayers have made predictions about imminent events in hundreds of ways, and many have based their predictions on the human body. Those who practiced onychomancy divined the future by studying the sun's reflection in the oiled fingernails of an innocent young boy. In ancient Greece some practiced

In ancient
Greece someone
who practiced
gastromancy
listened to wordlike
rumbles that issued
from a person's
stomach.

gastromancy, Greek for "belly prophecy." This involved listening to wordlike rumbles supposedly uttered from a person's stomach.

Beyond the body, prophets have pulled back the curtain of time by studying the stars, the flight patterns of birds, the shapes of puddles, and marks in the dirt. The future has been read in cards, numbers, names, and religious books. And soothsayers also have claimed to learn about the future directly from the gods through visions and dreams.

A Matter of Words

Prophecy is as old as humanity. A number of words are used to describe those who make prophecies, depending on which method is used to read the future. Those who study the stars and planets to foretell events are called astrologers. People who make predictions inspired by dreams, visions, or hallucinations might be called oracles, shamans, clairvoyants, psychics, or magicians. Those who practice the art of prophecy by reading flames in a fire are called pyromancers. *Soothsayer* is a term that first came into use in the fifteenth century when the word *truth* was also pronounced as "sooth" in Old English. A person who had the powers to predict the future was someone who spoke the truth, a truth-sayer, or soothsayer.

Playing a Significant Role

Soothsayers are often said to practice the art of divination, a term that derives from the Latin *divinare*. This means to be inspired by the gods or to discern the will of the gods. Soothsayers use divination to prophesy about major events affecting large groups of people. Their predictions deal with the destinies of cities, nations, and the entire planet. Historically, those who uttered prophecies made

Taking inspiration from the gods, soothsayers traditionally predicted, or prophesied, major world events such as floods, famines, or earthquakes—like the massive temblor that set off a deadly tsunami in Japan in March 2011 (pictured).

predictions about floods, famines, earthquakes, revolutions, wars, and other major events. This differs from the work of fortune-tellers, card readers, palm readers and others who make predictions about individuals, their loves, lives, and luck.

In centuries past, prophecy was practiced only among the most elite members of society. Soothsayers were employed by kings, queens, priests, generals, and other leaders to envision unknown dangers, unseen challenges, and hidden opportunities. Prophecies were sought 5,000 years ago by the pharaohs of

In the fifteenth
century the word
truth was also
pronounced as
"sooth," and a
person who spoke
the truth, a truth-
sayer, or soothsayer.

ancient Egypt and around the first century AD by Roman rulers. Some rulers banned prophecy among average citizens because it was seen as a threat to their power. For example, during China's Han dynasty in the third century BC, common methods of soothsaying were banned because prophecies often contradicted the official version of political events.

Controlling Uncertainties

Many soothsayers have been controversial, but their prophecies have captured the public imagination for centuries. Sixteenth-century soothsayer Nostradamus remains popular today because of his cryptic predictions made 500 years ago. In the twentieth century, self-proclaimed prophet Edgar Cayce developed a large following due to his predictions about cataclysmic events. Cayce's most notable prophecy concerned a major earthquake that would cause California to fall into the Pacific Ocean. In the twenty-first century, soothsayers and prophecies have gone digital. Countless websites focus on predictions concerning environmental calamities, the prospect of worldwide enlightenment, or the Apocalypse as predicted by the Bible.

Skeptics point out that people have been predicting the destruction of humanity for five millennia, yet people still exist. Major calamities do take place, but real disasters are rarely prophesied by soothsayers.

Life on Earth is uncertain. Almost everybody at some point wishes to see into the future when major decisions must be made. As long as the desire to control the uncontrollable remains, soothsayers will have a willing audience. People want to know what is going to happen in the coming year because the future is where everyone will spend the rest of their lives.

CHAPTER 1

Peering into the Future

O n March 14, 44 BC, a Roman soothsayer named Spurinnia killed a goat with a sacred knife. He sliced the animal open and pulled out the liver and intestines. After arranging the bloody mess on a special stone slab, Spurinnia studied the colors and shapes of the organs. The soothsayer said the organs revealed that Roman leader Julius Caesar would be murdered the following day on the ides of March (March 15). Caesar was warned but did not believe the soothsayer's prophecy, thinking it was the work of enemies trying to scare him.

Caesar expected to be named king of Rome on the ides of March, but Spurinnia's prophecy came true. Caesar was killed in the Roman senate when conspirators stabbed him 23 times. Roman statesman Cicero later wrote that Spurinnia had made a correct prophecy when studying the goat's entrails: "These

portents were sent by the immortal gods to Caesar that he might foresee his death, not that he might prevent it."[2]

Messages from the Gods

Like most others in the ancient world, Cicero believed the gods and goddesses controlled all events in the present and future. If the deities determined Caesar would die, nothing could be done to prevent the murder. As with crop failures, volcanic eruptions, and foreign invasions, assassinations were believed to be predetermined by the gods.

While the future was thought to be unchangeable, people also believed that gods and goddesses might reveal hints about forthcoming events. To do so, deities would manipulate animal entrails in a certain, specific way. The arrangement of the guts would disclose the gods' will to the soothsayer. The role of Spurinnia and other soothsayers was to interpret the divine messages.

Gods and goddesses could also communicate through vivid dreams. Some of the oldest examples of dream prophecy come from classical Greece, a culture that was flourishing around the fifth century BC. The Greeks believed that prophetic dreams were messages from the supreme god Zeus. The communications were delivered to mortals by Zeus's two sons: Morpheus, the god of dreams, and Hypnos, the god of sleep. However, Zeus was known as a fickle god. He might send dreams that contained prophecy, but he also might send messages meant to deceive the dreamer.

Because of the uncertain, symbolic nature of dreams, people often did not understand the prophecies being delivered by the gods. For example a person might dream about radishes, flying ants, or eating his own flesh. To determine the prophetic nature of such dreams, people visited soothsayers called dream readers.

The Dream Factory

The belief in prophetic dreams was so strong in ancient Greece that three elaborate shrines, called oracles, were built. Soothsayers worked in these shrines analyzing peoples' dreams. The most famous oracle was dedicated to Amphiaraus, a god-hero of Greek mythology. Amphiaraus was a legendary soothsayer given prophetic powers by Zeus. According to the second-century Greek author Pausanias, "Amphiaraus devoted himself most to the exposition of dreams. It is manifest that, when his divinity was established, it was a dream oracle that he set up."[3] The shrine of Amphiaraus, built in Oropos, a city 30 miles north of Athens, is called the Amphiareion of Oropos. Archaeologist Philipp Vandenberg calls the shrine a "dream-factory in which . . . people were sent to sleep

The ancient Roman soothsayer Spurinnia foretold the murder of Julius Caesar after extracting and examining the liver and intestines of a goat. Caesar refused to believe the prophecy, which came true, as depicted in this fifteenth-century painting.

for days and programmed to dream about the future."[4]

Visitors to the Amphiareion of Oropos included Greek noble-women, intellectuals, government officials, and soldiers. Clients slept in a large room, 350 feet (106m) long, together with more than 100 other patrons. According to Pausanias, visitors had to follow specific procedures to enter the dream factory: "One who has come to consult Amphiaraus is wont first to purify himself. The mode of purification is to sacrifice to the god [Amphiaraus]. . . . [They] sacrifice a ram, and, spreading the skin under them, go to sleep and await enlightenment in a dream."[5]

The sleepers were attended by specially trained dream readers. When people awoke in the middle of the night, soothsayers rushed over to ask about their dreams. As the groggy patrons struggled to remember the dream imagery, their words were written down on a tablet. The symbolic content of the dreams was explained along with any prophecies they might contain. The tablets were placed in storage. When soothsayers were called upon by rulers to prophecy about important future events, the stored dream tablets could be analyzed for clues into the desires of the deities.

The Oracle of Delphi

The Amphiareion was one among many shrines in ancient Greece dedicated to prophecy. The most famous oracle was established at the Temple of Apollo on Mount Parnassus at Delphi. The oracle of Delphi was used by the Greeks for nearly a thousand years, from the sixth century BC to the fourth century AD.

The Delphic oracle was located in a mountain cave. The entrance was marked by a gold statue of Apollo. Soothsayers at the shrine were women who had been picked by respected priests.

Every prophet at Delphi was named Pythia and wore a robe and a laurel crown. Pythia dispensed prophecies to people who believed she was acting as a mouthpiece for Apollo, son of Zeus. Apollo, the god of truth, light, music, poetry, and prophecy, was one of the most important Greek gods.

Kings, queens, nobles, and generals traveled hundreds of miles to consult with Pythia. Before seeing the oracle, prophecy seekers performed purification ceremonies and sacrificed bulls and goats to the gods. When they entered the cave, visitors' senses were overwhelmed. The shrine smelled of sweet perfume and burning incense. Pythia was paid with expensive cloth and rugs, jewelry, gold statues, fine dinnerware, and other treasures, which decorated every surface of the cave.

In the second century AD mathematician and philosopher Apollonius of Tyana described Pythia's reaction as she engaged in the art of prophecy: "[Pythia's] chest swelled; first she flushed, then paled; her limbs trembled convulsively and more and more violently. Her eyes seemed to flash fire; she foamed at the mouth; her hair stood on end. Then . . . she uttered a few words, which the priests at her side noted down."[6] Greek historian Herodotus had an explanation for these bizarre physical reactions. In the fourth century BC Herodotus wrote that cracks in the cave floor at Delphi emitted volcanic gases. This toxic cloud caused the Pythia to tremble, foam at the mouth, and hallucinate.

In 2001 the suspicions of Herodotus were confirmed. A team of geologists uncovered traces of a volcanic gas called ethylene, which has a sweet smell and produces a narcotic effect described as a floating or disembodied euphoria. Combined with the expectations of seekers this toxic gas may have inspired nearly 10 centuries of prophecy.

Did You Know?

The prophets at the oracle of Delphi were thought to be a mouthpiece for Apollo, the god of truth, light, music, poetry, and prophecy.

A Prophecy of Woe

One of the most famous prophecies to come from the oracle of Delphi concerns a war between Greece and Persia. In 480 BC Xerxes, the ruler of Persia, decided to invade Greece with an army that was the largest and most formidable in the world. As the Persian army closed in on Athens, a group of Greek leaders rushed to the Delphic oracle seeking advice. The men, led by a general named Themistocles, were startled when Pythia cried out distressing news:

> [All] is ruined, for fire and the headlong God of War
> Speeding in a [Persian] chariot shall bring you low,
> Many a tower shall he destroy, not yours alone,
> And give to pitiless fire many shrines of the gods.
> Which even now stand sweating, with fear quivering,
> While over the rooftops black blood runs streaming
> In prophecy of woe . . . bow your hearts in grief.[7]

After hearing this pronouncement, Themistocles told a local priest the terrible news. The man advised the general to return to Pythia with an offering of an olive branch, a symbol of peace. Asking the soothsayer for a better prophecy, Themistocles was rewarded. Pythia seemed to reverse herself, reciting cryptic verses that indicated the Greeks should abandon Athens in order to fight the Persians at sea. Backed by the prophecy from Delphi, Themistocles was able to convince citizens and soldiers to follow the plan. In one of the biggest sea battles in the history of the world at that time, the Greeks prevailed over a much larger fleet of Persian warships. However, Persian soldiers were able to burn Athens, and many a tower was destroyed as Pythia had predicted. But the citizens of the city were saved because they had fled on the advice of the soothsayer.

"Lions Will Die"

While few soothsayers crouch in caves in the modern era, other ancient tools of prophecy remain in use today. Among the most popular is astrology, followed by millions of people who read their daily horoscopes in newspapers, magazines, and online. Most modern astrological predictions are tailored to disclose events in the lives of individuals. However, soothsayers have been reading the stars for thousands of years to make major predictions about earth-shattering events.

People in ancient cultures believed that the deities could arrange the stars and planets in patterns that would reveal the future, much as they did with goat entrails. This concept was first explored around 3100 BC by the ancient Babylonians who lived in what is now called Iraq. Babylonian priests and soothsayers mapped and named stars using 700 symbols in the first formalized system of writing, called cuneiform.

By 2000 BC Babylonian soothsayers had compiled a massive number of clay tablets imprinted with astrological prophecies. These omens were compiled into a work known as *Enuna Anu Enlil* sometime around 1600 BC and were used by soothsayers for more than a 1,000 years. The 70 clay tablets contained at least 7,000 omens, or prophecies, based on the positions of the sun, moon, planets, stars, and the timing of eclipses. The omens, thought to be directed by the gods, had a direct influence on kings, nobility, and entire nations. In one prophecy from the *Enuna Anu Enlil*, great importance was placed on the appearance of a halo around the moon, which is now known to be caused by moisture in the atmosphere. The halo prophesied bad omens when the moon was in the sign of Scorpio and Jupiter nearby in the sky. According to the *Enuna Anu Enlil*, "When a halo surrounds the Moon and Jupiter stands within it, the King . . . will

be besieged. When a halo surrounds the Moon and Jupiter stands within it, there will be a slaughter of cattle and beasts of the field. . . . When a halo surrounds the Moon and Scorpio stands in it . . . lions will die."[8]

An Instrument of Power

In later centuries the classical Greeks perfected the ancient system of astrology devised by the Babylonians. The methods the Greeks used to cast horoscopes have changed little over the centuries and are still in use. Today, as in ancient Greece, when a baby is born, astrologers determine the exact location of the sun, moon, and planets at that moment. Soothsayers used the same information to predict major events. After Greek culture was absorbed by the Romans around the first century BC, astrology divided along two paths. Common citizens had their horoscopes drawn up by amateur diviners at street markets and carnivals. Powerful Roman emperors came to rely on court astrologers. The prophecies of these soothsayers exerted great influence over the affairs of the Roman state.

Augustus, who ruled from 27 BC to AD 14, was the first emperor of the Roman Empire. He relied heavily on astrologers to make major decisions. Augustus's interest in astrology might be traced to a prediction made by the astrologer Theogenes. It was allegedly made 20 years before Augustus became emperor. The historian Suetonius describes the prophecy about Augustus and his friend Agrippa who would later become a famous statesman and general:

> Augustus and Agrippa together visited the house of Theogenes the astrologer . . . to consult him about their future careers. Agrippa went first, and

In ancient Greece, kings and queens, nobles, and generals traveled hundreds of miles to consult with the Oracle of Delphi (pictured). Believers attributed the Delphic oracle's prophecies to Apollo, son of Zeus and god of truth, light, and prophecy.

he was prophesied with such almost incredible good fortune that Augustus expected a far less encouraging response, and felt ashamed to disclose the time of his birth. Yet when at last, after a great deal of hesitation, he grudgingly supplied the information . . . Theogenes rose and flung himself at his feet; and this gave Augustus so implicit a faith in his destiny that he even ventured to publish his horoscope, and struck a silver coin stamped with [Augustus's birth sign] Capricorn.[9]

"[Pythia's] eyes seemed to flash fire; she foamed at the mouth; her hair stood on end. Then . . . she uttered a few words, which the priests at her side noted down."

—Greek historian Herodotus, describing the Oracle of Delphi.

The story of Theogenes's prediction could have easily been made up after Augustus became emperor in order to justify his rise to power. If it was, it demonstrates the role of astrology in ancient Rome. Even a powerful ruler like Augustus needed to prove that the stars had blessed his ascension to the throne.

While Augustus used astrology to legitimize his reign, other emperors used it as a tool of oppression. Tiberius ruled after Augustus and often stayed on the island of Capri surrounded by an influential group of soothsayers. These men studied the stars and used prophecy to identify the political enemies of Tiberius. Those named were immediately arrested and murdered. However, even the astrologers themselves could fall victim to Tiberius's capriciousness. Tiberius took joy in testing the soothsayers by making them foretell the time of their own deaths. While the soothsayers often predicted they would die some decades in the future, Tiberius would then prove them wrong by executing them on the spot.

Advisers to Nobles and Prominent People

The importance of astrology was greatly diminished after the collapse of the Roman Empire in the fifth century. The Christian Church became the most powerful institution in Europe, and religious leaders accused astrologers and soothsayers of heresy. Anyone convicted of heresy, or holding beliefs contrary to church teachings, could be burned at the stake. Despite official prohibition of the practice, the belief in the predictive powers of astrology remained strong among some nobles. As religious scholar Max Jacobi writes: "Towards the close of the Middle Ages [around 1450] nearly every petty prince, as well as every ruler of importance, had his court astrologer upon whose ambiguous utterances the [welfare] and the woe of the whole country often depended."[10]

During the sixteenth century, astrology was a major field of study for several renowned astronomers and mathematicians. For example, Johannes Kepler, who accurately described the orbital paths of planets around the sun in 1609, also made astrological prophecies for Austrian emperor Rudolf II. Perhaps the most famous mathematician and astronomer of the age, Italian scientist Galileo, often gave astrological advice to distinguished people.

Galileo proved that the Earth orbits around the sun and discovered several moons of Jupiter in 1610. During this period he also acted as an official astronomer to his young patron, Cosimo de' Medici, the Duke of Tuscany. Jupiter played an extremely important role in Cosimo's life, according to Galileo:

> So who does not know that . . . kindness of heart, gentleness of manners, splendor of royal blood, nobleness in public functions, wide extent of influence and power over others, all of which [are found] in your highness—who, I say, does not know that these qualities . . . emanate from the most benign star of Jupiter?[11]

Galileo used his powers of astrological prophecy to advise other members of the esteemed Medici family. And while the church officially condemned astrology, Galileo was called upon by Roman Catholic cardinal Alessandro d'Este to make prophecies based on the positions of the planets and stars.

The President's Astrologer

Powerful people continued to consult astrologers well into the modern age. One of the most recent examples was revealed in the

"[Nearly] every petty prince, as well as every ruler of importance, had his court astrologer upon whose ambiguous utterances the [welfare] and the woe of the whole country often depended."

—Religious scholar Max Jacobi, describing the importance of astrology in fifteenth-century Europe.

Astrology and Skepticism

Unlike the ancient Babylonians who founded astrology, scientists today understand that stars are billions of miles from Earth. Their positions change over the centuries, and the stars in familiar astrological constellations, such as Pisces, Virgo, and Libra, are all millions of miles away from one another. In an article excerpted below, British biologist Richard Dawkins points out that astrology denies this basic scientific concept and is therefore a "wicked fraud":

> On a moonless night . . . go out to a place far from street light pollution, lie on the grass and gaze out at the stars. What are you seeing? Superficially you

late 1980s. According to newspaper accounts at the time, President Ronald Reagan relied on California astrologer Joan Quigley for more than seven years. Quigley was hired by First Lady Nancy Reagan after a failed 1981 assassination attempt on the president.

notice constellations, but a constellation is of no more significance than a patch of curiously shaped [mold] on the bathroom ceiling. [Constellations are] miscellaneous sets of stars all at different distances from us, which have no connection with each other except that they constitute a (meaningless) pattern when seen from a certain place in the galaxy (here). A constellation is not an entity at all. . . . The shape of a constellation, moreover, is [temporary]. . . . A million years hence, our descendants will see . . . other shapes in the sky, and their astrologers will be fabricating their [prophecies] on the basis of a different zodiac.

Richard Dawkins, "The Real Romance in the Stars," Astrological Association of Great Britain, 2010. www.astrologer.com.

Quigley told the First Lady she could have foreseen and possibly prevented the threat.

After Quigley went to work for the Reagans, she created a horoscope for the United States. This was based on the belief

"Not since the days of the Roman emperors—and never in the history of the United States Presidency—has an astrologer played such a significant role in the nation's affairs of State."

—Joan Quigley, President Ronald Reagan's astrologer.

that the country's "birthday" was July 4, 1776, the date traditionally celebrated as the day of independence. Quigley spent her days creating astrological charts based on the daily movements of the stars and planets. These were compared with Reagan's birth chart and the horoscope she created for the United States. The information provided a basis for prophecies concerning presidential speeches, travel, and press conferences.

Quigley was called upon to decide the exact minute that the presidential plane, *Air Force One,* would take off. She also advised the president on major decisions. When Reagan wished to announce he was seeking reelection in early December 1983, Quigley said the timing was terrible. She convinced the president to wait until January 29, and then to make the speech at 10:55 p.m., a late hour that caused a great deal of wonder in the news media. Quigley even advised Reagan about signing a 1987 treaty with the Soviet Union that banned a certain class of nuclear missiles. The astrologer later commented on her role: "Not since the days of the Roman emperors—and never in the history of the United States Presidency—has an astrologer played such a significant role in the nation's affairs of State."[12]

In 1988 a book by White House chief of staff Donald Regan revealed that the president relied on an astrologer. This caused the First Lady great embarrassment and Quigley was immediately fired. However, those who believed in prophecies and soothsayers could not condemn the president. He was following a tradition that was thousands of years old. Modern presidents face some of the same threats as did ancient Roman emperors. With no scientific method for prophesying, astrology, dreams, and even animal entrails are, for now, the only way soothsayers can see into the uncertain future.

CHAPTER 2

Prophecies and the Bible

The Bible is considered the most important theological work for Christians worldwide. It is composed of 66 chapters, called books, and divided into two sections, the Old Testament and the New Testament. Predictions made by prophets appear in both sections, and biblical prophecies have influenced world affairs for thousands of years.

The Old Testament, also called the Hebrew Bible, is arranged in three sections known as the Law, the Prophets, and the Writings. The section called the Prophets features books concerned with three major prophets, Isaiah, Jeremiah, Ezekiel, and twelve minor prophets including Joel, Amos, Jonah, and Micah.

The Old Testament prophets had a special relationship with God, who either spoke to them directly or showed the future in visions. This occurred when the prophets were in a state of

mental and spiritual ecstasy. As theologian Stephen F. Winward explains: "In this condition the prophet ceased to be aware of the ordinary circumstances and relationships of life and became intensely aware of God. The personality of the prophet was . . . raised to a new intensity through the encounter with God, and [the prophet] became the medium for divine revelation."[13]

Lamentation and Mourning

The prophet Ezekiel, believed to have lived in the sixth century BC, had an intense encounter with God, described in great detail in the Bible. Around 592 BC, when Ezekiel was about 30 years old, he had an amazingly vivid vision when a bright storm cloud approached. Lightning filled the sky, and the heavens opened up, revealing four living angels. According to the Book of Ezekiel, chapter 1, verses 5–11 written as 1:5–11:

> Each of [the angels] had four faces and four wings.
>
> Their legs were straight and their feet were like a calf's hoof, and they gleamed like burnished bronze.
>
> Under their wings on their four sides were human hands. As for the faces and wings of the four of them, their wings touched one another; their faces did not turn when they moved, each went straight forward.
>
> As for the form of their faces, each had the face of a man; all four had the face of a lion on the right and

the face of a bull on the left, and all four had the face of an eagle.

Such were their faces. Their wings were spread out above; each had two touching another being, and two covering their bodies.

Next to the angels Ezekiel sees four wheels with spokes that seem like wheels within wheels that contain "the spirit of the living creatures." The angels and the wheels support a solid platform that shine like crystal. A fantastic throne appears, and God, a figure of indescribable brightness and majesty, is seated upon it. As the Bible states, God hands Ezekiel a scroll with words of "lamentation and mourning and woe."

After receiving the prophecy from God, Ezekiel is able to visualize what is happening in Jerusalem although he is hundreds of miles away. He has several intense visions in which he sees Jerusalem as a "bloody city" where bribery, extortion, and corruption are rampant. Ezekiel prophesies the total destruction of Jerusalem by Nebuchadnezzar, the king of Babylon. This event comes to pass five years after Ezekiel's first encounter with God.

"Turn or Burn" Prophecies

Ezekiel was able to prophesy about events that took place in the foreseeable future. Like the other prophets in the Old Testament, Ezekiel did not make predictions about events that would take place in a hundred or a thousand years. Instead, Old Testament prophets received direct revelations from God about what He would do in the coming days, months, or years. These prophecies were often used to warn people that they must improve their behavior. If they did not repent, God would destroy them, usually with an invading army. As Bible scholar Steven L. McKenzie explains: "[The prophets'] pronouncements about the future were not so much predictions as threats. Theirs was a 'turn or burn' message: 'This is what will happen to you if you do not change your ways.'"[14]

The Old Testament "turn or burn" prophecies often held out hope for the future. If the predicted destruction took place, the prophecy implied that the calamity would be overcome someday. As the religion scholar Tom McIver explains, "The evil order [would be] violently destroyed, and after this destruction, a Golden Age lay ahead for righteous believers, an age outside of history."[15] For example, after Jerusalem was destroyed, as Ezekiel had prophesied, Jeremiah has a revelation that the Babylonian captivity would end in 70 years. The Bible says this prophecy came to pass after 68 years, and a flowering of Jewish culture took place in Jerusalem.

Revealing the Apocalypse

The New Testament contains many "turn or burn" prophecies, but the Bible ends with predictions of a coming Apocalypse. The New Testament does not give an exact time when total destruction will take place. Jesus states that the end is "not yet," and "no man knows the day or hour" of the Apocalypse. Many events needed to take place before the End Times, and they include wars and rumors of war, conflict between nations, famines and earthquakes, an increase in wickedness, and the martyrdom of Christians.

The word *apocalypse* is derived from the ancient Greek *apokalupsis*, which means "unveiling," or "revelation." The apocalyptic

According to the Old Testament, the prophet Ezekiel (pictured here in Michelangelo's Sistine Chapel painting) prophesied the destruction of Jerusalem after experiencing a revelation from God. The event later came to pass just as Ezekiel foretold.

prophecies in the Bible are written in the last chapter, appropriately named the Book of Revelation.

As Revelation begins the reader is informed that the message contained within was given to Jesus Christ by God. Jesus revealed the prophecies to someone named John who lived on the small Greek island of Patmos around AD 95. Scholars disagree over

John's identity. Some believe he was the Apostle John, one of the disciples of Jesus who wrote several books of the New Testament including the fourth Gospel. Others believe John was another person, referred to as John of Patmos. Whoever he was, John enters a visionary state in Revelation in which he is transported to heaven. There the prophecies are revealed through a series of images and events concerning the final Apocalypse on Earth.

The deliverance of prophecies to John begins with a loud blast, like a trumpet. He hears a voice that commands him to write down all he is about to see "of present happenings and things that are still to come!" (1:17–19). These visions are recorded in letters by John and sent to seven Greek churches in seven cities that include Smyrna, Ephesus, and Sardis, all located in Asia Minor, or modern western Turkey.

The number seven plays prominently in Revelation. After hearing the commands from behind, John turns and sees Jesus surrounded by seven gold lamp-stands (candlesticks) and holding seven stars in his right hand. John is informed that the seven stars represent angels of the seven Greek churches and the lamp-stands symbolize the churches themselves. This imagery is taken directly from the Old Testament prophet Zechariah who had a vision of a gold lamp-stand with seven lamps, or candles, in the Temple of Jerusalem. These are said to represent the seven known heavenly bodies at the time, the five planets with the sun and moon.

As Revelation continues, John sees a sharp, double-edged sword extend from the mouth of Jesus. John faints in terror but is revived by Jesus. The narrative continues as John ascends through a door that opens up in the heavens. A voice informs John he is about to see "what is to come in the future" (4:1). John now has a vision similar to that of Ezekiel. Amid cacophonous thunder and bolts of lightning, God appears on a throne surrounded by seven angels and four creatures resembling a lion, a bull, a human, and an eagle. Each has six wings and eyes all around the head.

The Seven Seals

John is shown a scroll sealed with seven seals. One by one the seals are opened by Jesus, represented as the Lamb with seven horns and seven eyes, "which are the seven Spirits of God sent forth into all the earth" (6:1). Each seal makes known a prophecy of a specific apocalyptic disaster. The first four seals bring forth horses and riders, known as the Four Horsemen of the Apocalypse. When the first seal is broken, a white horse of pestilence, or a deadly plague, appears. The second seal brings forth a fiery red horse of war. According to John: "Its rider was given power to take peace from the earth and to make men slay each other. To him was given a large sword" (6:3).

When the third seal is opened a black horse of famine appears. The vision following the fourth seal's opening is described by John: "I looked, and there before me was a pale horse! Its rider was named Death, and [he was] given power over a fourth of the earth to kill by sword, famine and plague, and by the wild beasts of the earth" (6:7).

The opening of the fifth seal reveals the souls of all martyrs who have been executed for their belief in God. They cry for revenge. When the sixth seal is cracked, a massive earthquake rocks the planet. The sky is blackened with volcanic ash, the moon turns as red as blood, and the stars fall out of the sky. Every person on Earth, rich or poor, prince or slave, tries to hide in caves and between the rocks of mountains because each knows the day of reckoning has arrived. The destruction is halted temporarily

Mark of the Beast

People have debated the meaning of the Mark of the Beast and the significance of the number 666 for centuries. Some historians believe the meaning of 666 can be traced to the way numbers and letters were used in an interchangeable manner in the first century AD when John wrote Revelation. At the time, Greek and Hebrew writers used specific numbers to represent individual letters. For example, the letter "n" represented the number 200, the letter "r" was also a symbol for 60. By applying numbers to the letters in a name and adding them all together, a larger number

so that God may place seals upon the foreheads of all righteous believers. These people include 12,000 of the faithful from each of the 12 tribes of Israel, or 144,000 in all.

Before the Lamb opens the seventh seal, an ominous silence falls for 30 minutes. When this ends, seven angels sound seven trumpets announcing a series of seven disasters. The first trumpet brings hail and fire which destroys one-third of all vegetation

appeared. This system has been applied to the name of the Roman emperor Nero, who ruled from AD 54 to 68. Nero was seen as a tyrant by Christians like John, and the emperor might havebeen viewed as the Antichrist. The numbers in Nero's name add up to 666.

Many centuries later, in the 1600s, Protestants associated the number 666 with the pope. When the letters in the pope's title, *Vicarius Filii Dei* or Vicar of the Son of God, are translated into Roman numerals, they add up to 666. In modern times, the Mark of the Beast has been associated with social security numbers, which are required for all Americans who "buy and sell." Others have associated 666 with computer codes, various presidents, world leaders, and any other number, mark, or system that might identify Satan.

on the Earth. At the second trumpet, a mountain falls into the sea turning one-third of the water to blood, killing one-third of all sea creatures and destroying one-third of all ships. The third trumpet causes a star to fall from heaven and destroy one-third of all rivers. At the sound of the fourth trumpet, the heavenly bodies collide and one-third of the Earth's light from the sun, moon, and stars is lost.

The Woe Trumpets

In the prophecy, the last three trumpets are called the Woe Trumpets because, John writes, "Woe! woe! woe! to those dwelling on the earth as a result of the rest of the soundings of the trumpets of the three messengers who are about to be trumpeting!" (8:13).

The fifth trumpet brings judgment from beneath as a bottomless pit opens. Clouds of smoke pour out teeming with locusts that possess human faces and scorpion tails. These hideous insects torture all those without God's seal for five months. When the sixth trumpet sounds, 200 million horsemen emerge to kill one-third of humankind.

When the seventh trumpet sounds, it is time for God to unleash his wrath on nonbelievers. The dramatic prophecy begins with John's vision of Jesus as a child in the sky with a woman, the Virgin Mary who is, "adorned with the sun, standing on the moon, and with twelve stars on her head for a crown" (12:1–2). A monstrous red Dragon with ten horns and seven heads tries to eat the child but is challenged by the archangel Michael and other angels. A battle ensues between the angels and the Dragon. As the angels defeat the Dragon and cast him down to Earth, Jesus is taken to heaven for protection. The angry Dragon does not disappear, however. Instead, it is revealed to be Satan, a force of evil unleashed upon the world to meddle in the lives of believers.

The Day of the Beast

At this point in Revelation, Jesus is in heaven with God, Mary is safe, and Satan has been cast out of heaven by the angels. But the prophecies do not stop. The most frightening and disturbing visions of the future continue with John beginning, "I was standing on the sand of the sea" (13:1). This is the last moment of peace for John, who continues: "And I perceived a wild beast ascending out

A 2010 Gallup
poll states that
about one-third of
American adults
believe the Bible is
absolutely accurate
and that it should be
taken literally, word
for word.

of the sea, having ten horns and seven heads." This beast has features resembling a bear, leopard, and lion and is later identified by John as Satan, the symbol of all that is evil. In later centuries, the satanic beast came to be referred to as the Antichrist, although this term is never mentioned in Revelation.

A second beast emerges from the earth with two horns like a lamb but speaking like a dragon. The land beast is a servant to the sea beast with seven heads. The new beast builds a statue of the sea beast, breathing life into it and making it talk. The land beast performs miracles that force the world to worship Satan.

The land beast demands "the rich and the poor, and the free and the slaves, the small and the great" receive Satan's emblem, later called the Mark of the Beast, on the right hand or forehead. Without the mark, no one can buy or sell. Then John prophesies, "Let him who has a mind calculate the number of the sea beast [Satan], for it is the number of mankind, and its number is six hundred sixty-six." (13:16–18).

Three angels fly by. The first preaches the Gospel to the world, the second announces that Babylon has fallen, and third explains that all who accept the Mark of the Beast, or 666, are doomed. They will be tortured by the angels forever and ever. But all who resist the mark and are martyred will be blessed and rewarded by God. Then John has a vision of Jesus wearing a gold crown and casting grapes into a winepress representing God's wrath. Blood runs from the winepress and fills the earth 6 feet (2m) deep.

King of Kings

The nightmarish prophecies of Revelation continue when angels bring forth seven plagues from seven bowls. Some of the plagues include excessive heat from the sun, oceans turning to blood, and nonbelievers stricken with horrible, malignant sores. The sixth bowl dries up the Euphrates River, which allows armies from the east to march into Israel. The soldiers, led by Satan, prepare for a world war. Upon the pouring of the seventh bowl, a voice from heaven cries, "The end has come," as a great earthquake and huge hailstones destroy Rome and other cities. The narrative turns to a great battle between good and evil. As John prophesies, the forces of good appear:

> I saw heaven standing open and there before me was a white horse, whose rider is called Faithful and True. With justice he judges and wages war. His eyes are like blazing fire, and on his head are many crowns. . . . He is dressed in a robe dipped in blood, and his name is the Word of God. The armies of heaven were following him, riding on white horses and dressed in fine linen, white and clean. . . . On his robe and on his thigh he has this name written: KING OF KINGS AND LORD OF LORDS (19:11–16).

The forces of good are met by Satan and the land beast, now called the False Prophet. These forces of evil are thrown live into a fiery lake of burning sulfur. Satan is imprisoned in the Abyss, a bottomless pit, for 1,000 years, and, as John writes, "they shall be tormented day or night for ever and ever" (20:10).

God now appears on his throne, and all who have ever died are resurrected and judged. Nonbelievers and sinners are cast into the lake of fire with Satan. The prophecies end when Jesus and his

"[The prophets'] pronouncements about the future were not so much predictions as threats. Theirs was a 'turn or burn' message."

—Bible scholar Steven L. McKenzie.

followers reign in New Jerusalem, a "new heaven and a new earth," where there is no death, sorrow, suffering, or uncleanness.

John's vision of New Jerusalem is extremely detailed. He provides exact dimensions of the city and the great wall around it. He describes buildings made of pure gold garnished with precious stones such as jasper, sapphire, emerald, topaz, and amethyst. John concludes Revelation with these words: "For I testify unto every man that heareth the words of the prophecy of this book, if any man shall add unto these things, God shall add unto him the plagues that are written in this book. . . . He which testifieth these things saith, Surely I come quickly. Amen (22:18–20).

Past, Present, and Future

Over the centuries, John's prophecies in Revelation have been interpreted in many different, complex, confusing, and contradictory ways. One school of thought, associated with Roman Catholicism, is called preterism. This theory about Revelation, developed in the seventeenth century, holds that almost all of the prophecies in the book happened in the first century after Christ's birth. Preterism is based on the idea that Revelation describes divine judgment on the Jews for rejecting the teachings of Jesus. The prophecies were fulfilled when Roman soldiers destroyed Jerusalem in 70 AD. In this view, Revelation is not a judgment on the entire world that will take place in the distant future, but applies only to the Jewish people of ancient times.

Another viewpoint, associated with Protestant thought, is called historicism. This concept holds that some of the prophecies have already taken place, while others will be fulfilled in the coming years.

Those who believe that Revelation describes events that have not yet taken place are called futurists. These people tend to think that Revelation is literal, in that events will unfold exactly as John described them. Others believe that John's prophecies are symbolic, representing a parable or story that represents a general struggle between good and evil.

While all agree John's prophecies were written in the first century, they have been used by futurists for nearly 2,000 years to predict what is known as the End Times. In the twentieth century some claimed that Revelation predicted the destruction of World Wars I and II and events that might have caused a nuclear war between the United States and the Soviet Union. In 2001 some claimed the terrorist attack on the World Trade Center fulfilled prophecies in Revelation.

In recent years hundreds of websites have put forth the idea that the prophecies in Revelation are happening or are about to happen. According to these sites, various leaders have allegedly been branded with 666, the Mark of the Beast. These people include Pope Benedict XVI, presidents George W. Bush and Barack Obama, and even Microsoft founder and billionaire Bill Gates.

Widespread Belief

Millions of people throughout the world fully believe in the concept of the End Times as described in Revelation. A 2010 Gallup poll states that about one-third of American adults believe the Bible is absolutely accurate and that it should be taken literally, word for word. However, the exact meaning of John's prophecies are open to debate, and his words are often misquoted, misinterpreted, or taken out of context. Whatever their true meaning, the prophecies of John, written thousands of years ago, continue to resonate in a world that has changed beyond measure since ancient times.

CHAPTER 3

Nostradamus

On September 11, 2001, four jet airliners were highjacked by terrorists. Two of the planes smashed into the 110-story Twin Towers of the World Trade Center (WTC) in New York City at speeds approaching 600 miles per hour (965kph). Another was flown into the Pentagon, headquarters for the US military in Washington, DC. The fourth airplane crashed into a field in Pennsylvania. Within two hours the World Trade Center skyscrapers collapsed into rubble. Nearly 3,000 people died in the attacks that horrible day.

Within hours of the terrorist strike, the name Nostradamus appeared on anonymous e-mails that circled the globe. The e-mail messages made it seem as if the French soothsayer, who lived in the sixteenth century, had predicted the surprise attack. Lines attributed to Nostradamus stated:

> Two steel birds will fall from the sky on the Metropolis.
> The sky will burn at forty-five degrees latitude.

Smoke and flames pour from the World Trade Center in New York City after a 2001 terrorist attack. Within hours of the attack e-mails began circulating around the globe claiming that the sixteenth-century soothsayer Nostradamus had prophesied this event.

Fire approaches the great new city
Immediately a huge, scattered flame leaps up.
Within months, rivers will flow with blood.
The undead will roam earth for little time.[16]

New York City, sometimes called Metropolis, is located at 41° latitude, not "forty-five degrees." However, the quote attributed to Nostradamus eerily predicted the attack and the war in Afghanistan that followed.

Skeptics immediately noticed a problem with the six-line poem attributed to Nostradamus. It was dated 1645. Despite the French soothsayer's alleged powers of prophecy, it is doubtful he could have made the prediction in 1645. Nostradamus died in 1566.

The quote about steel birds and rivers of blood was soon shown to be a hoax. It was actually a misquoting of a real prediction by Nostradamus:

> At forty-five degrees the sky will burn
> Fire to approach the great new city:
> In an instant a great scattered flame will leap up. . . .
> Ruin . . . so very terrible with fear,
> Their great city stained, pestilential dead:
> To plunder the Sun and Moon and to violate their temples:
> And to redden the two rivers flowing with blood.[17]

Believers said that the prophecy applied because "two rivers" were the Hudson and East Rivers that flow around Manhattan. However, skeptics pointed out that the verses could have predicted any war in any city where two rivers flowed.

Plagues and Persecution

While believers and skeptics argue over the cryptic writings of Nostradamus, one fact remains. When disaster strikes, even in the twenty-first century, the name of a soothsayer who has been dead for more than 435 years will appear once again. Perhaps this is not surprising since Nostradamus is one of the most famous soothsayers who ever lived, and much is known about his life—the house where he was born in the town of St. Rémy, France, still stands. More important, the 10 books of prophecies called *Centuries*, written by Nostradamus between 1555 and 1557, have never been out of print. These volumes, now published in one book, contain dozens of world events prophesied to occur before 3797, the year Nostradamus said the world will end.

Michel de Nostredame was born in 1503. *Nostredame* means "our lady," and the soothsayer called himself Nostradamus, the Latinized version of his name. Nostradamus descended from a long line of physicians. His father and both his grandfathers were doctors to French nobles. Despite their positions, the family faced constant danger.

The Nostredames were Jewish, and two years after Nostradamus was born, King Louis XII ordered all French Jews to be baptized as Catholics or face expulsion or execution. Like many Jews of the time, the Nostredame family publically converted to Catholicism but continued to practice their faith in secret.

In this superstitious era, Jews were blamed for causing the black plague, which covers a victim's skin in ugly black pustules. Beginning in the 1340s, a black plague pandemic swept across Europe on a regular basis, leaving millions of dead in its wake.

The Innovative Doctor

Nostradamus was extremely intelligent and was schooled by his grandfather, Pierre de Nostredame. Nostradamus learned Hebrew, Greek, Latin, philosophy, mathematics, and medicine, but his favorite subject was astrology. At the age of 17, when he

"[Nostradamus would] slip into a trance of ecstasy where he heard and saw visions of his inner oracle boil from the waters of the brass bowl."

—Scholar John Hogue, describing the prophecy techniques of Nostradamus.

attended college at Avignon, the small-framed Nostradamus was nicknamed "the little astrologer"[18] by his classmates.

Astrology was considered an impractical career, so Nostradamus attended medical school in 1522. Three years later, at the age of 22, he became a doctor. When he received his medical license, a new outbreak of the black plague was devastating southern France. Nostradamus quickly went to work visiting patients. Nostradamus bravely entered disease-stricken cities such as Aix, Toulouse, and Bordeaux. He ordered corpses removed and the streets cleaned. Those who were not yet stricken with plague were told to bathe, drink plenty of water, and sit in the sunshine. His treatments seemed to help, and the plague receded in these cities.

A Wandering Soothsayer

During the 1530s Nostradamus was widely believed to have saved entire towns from the black plague. This led him to gain considerable recognition among the upper classes and royals. Because of this fame, one of Europe's most respected scholars, Julius-Cesar Scalinger, requested a meeting with Nostradamus in 1534. The two educated men discussed magic, astrology, philosophy, and other esoteric lore and soon became close friends. Scalinger lived in Agen and convinced Nostradamus to set up a practice in the small village. Soon after, Nostradamus married a woman whose name has been lost to history. However, she was described by Nostradamus biographer Jean Aimes de Chavigny as a woman "of high estate, very beautiful and very amiable."[19] The couple had two children, a son and a daughter. However, in 1537 plague struck Agen and Nostradamus's wife and children became gravely ill. Although he did everything in his power to cure them, Nostradamus was forced to watch helplessly as his family perished.

While Nostradamus was grieving over his loss, some of his most important supporters turned on him and blamed him for the tragedy. The doctor was abandoned by his wealthy patients and denounced by Scalinger. Fearing he would be arrested by church authorities for sorcery, Nostradamus left Agen in the middle of the night. For six years he wandered anonymously in Italy and France. During this period, Nostradamus is said to have honed his powers as a soothsayer, consulting with astrologers, magicians, fortune-tellers, and philosophers.

Although Nostradamus's travels are undocumented, one legend from this period was later recounted by Chavigny. In 1538 Nostradamus saw a humble monk walking down the road. The soothsayer bowed and humbly addressed him as "Your Holiness," a title reserved for the pope. In 1585 that monk, Felice Peretti, became Pope Sixtus V—19 years after Nostradamus's death.

A Trance of Ecstasy

Nostradamus returned to France in 1544 while the plague was once again ravaging entire regions. In some cities corpses were piled in the streets and neighborhoods stood empty after all residents succumbed to disease. Nostradamus, now 41 years old, visited these devastated places. He administered his herbal cures to hundreds while ordering them to bathe. These treatments were credited with stopping the plague in Salon, and grateful city leaders gave Nostradamus a pension for life. In 1547 he married a rich widow, Anne Posart Gemelle, and set up a laboratory in her home. There, working deep into the night, Nostradamus pursued his true passions, studying magic and astrology and writing prophecies.

One of the most famous soothsayers that ever lived, Nostradamus published almanacs filled with prophecies. The tools of his trade included astrological charts, herbal potions, and a magic wand.

To see into the future, Nostradamus assembled an array of forbidden magic books and instruments that were deemed satanic by the church. Among his tools were astrological charts, chemist's tools for creating herbal potions, and a magic wand. The soothsayer's most powerful tool is believed to have been a brass bowl filled with water. Nostradamus used this for a prophetic activity known as scrying, in which a soothsayer gazes into a shiny surface to envision prophecies. The process is described by Nostradamus scholar John Hogue:

[Nostradamus would sit] before a brass bowl filled with water to the brim. He would empty himself of thought and care by staring into a thin [candle] flame. He would then slip into a trance of ecstasy where he heard and saw visions of his inner oracle boil from the waters of the brass bowl. The images of what would be were dominated by visions of religious war coming soon to France.[20]

Beginning in 1550, Nostradamus began publishing annual almanacs filled with the prophecies for the coming year. The thin booklets also contained astrological information and advertisements for herbal cosmetics and drugs Nostradamus created in his spare time. One almanac contained a prophetic vision meant to cure ill health and disease. Nostradamus told people to boil water before drinking it. While it is now known that boiling water kills dangerous, disease-causing pathogens, this was not common knowledge until the late nineteenth century.

The almanacs of Nostradamus were an instant success and sold out quickly. The most popular section of the almanac was a chapter featuring prophecies written in four-line poems called quatrains. Each almanac had 12 quatrains, one for every month of the coming year. These predictions attracted admirers to Salon from near and far. One of Nostradamus's devotees was Chavigny, who stayed on to become the soothsayer's secretary. Chavigny later wrote the biography of Nostradamus that is still quoted today.

Writing *Centuries*

In early 1554 Nostradamus decided to undertake a project that would ensure his legacy as one of the world's greatest prophesiers. The books, now called *Centuries*, predicted humanity's future until the end of time in 3797.

To write the 10 volumes, Nostradamus prophesied every night. For months he consulted astrological charts and went into deep trances to scry. The morning after each session, Nostradamus would write down his prophecies or dictate them to Chavigny. The first books, *Centuries 1* through part of *4* were published in 1555. The rest of *4* and *Centuries 5* through *7* were published later, and all 10 were available by 1557. The books contained 942 predictions in all.

All Is Regulated and Governed

Nostradamus explaines his powers of prophecy in the preface to *Centuries*, which he dedicated to his young son Caesar:

> Events of human origin are uncertain, but all is regulated and governed by the incalculable power of God, inspiring us not through drunken fury, nor by frantic movement, but through the influences of the stars. Only those divinely inspired can predict particular things in a prophetic spirit.

Nostradamus feared his prophecies would lead church authorities to accuse him of sorcery, a capital crime. Punishment for this crime was burning at the stake. To protect himself, Nostradamus wrote *Centuries* using language that was obscure and difficult to decipher.

For a long time I have been making predictions, far in advance, of events since come to pass, naming the particular locality. I acknowledge that all to have been accomplished through divine power and inspiration. Predicted events, both happy and sad, have come to pass throughout the world with increased promptness. However, because of the possibility of harm, both for the present and most of the future, I became willing to keep silent and refrain from putting them into writing.

Quoted in Edgar Leoni, *Nostradamus and His Prophecies.* New York: Bell, 1982, p. 121.

The quatrains were written in Latin, Greek, and Old French, a language that was antiquated even in the sixteenth century. In addition the soothsayer invented words and inserted anagrams, words formed by reordering the letters of meaningful words or phrases.

"A Cruel Death"

In the preface to *Centuries*, Nostradamus writes that he did not want to tell all he knows of the future because it would upset the powerful, what he calls those of the present "kingdoms, sects, religions, and faiths."[21] Despite his attempts at obscurity, many were offended. Church leaders said Nostradamus was an instrument of Satan and his words were gibberish from hell. Doctors were embarrassed by their fellow physician while famous poets laughed at the perplexing verses in the quatrains. However, one of the prophecies caught the eye of Catherine de Médici, the queen of France:

> The young lion will overcome the older one,
> in a field of combat in single fight:
> He will pierce his eyes in their golden cage;
> two wounds in one, then he dies a cruel death.[22]

Catherine believed that the older lion in the quatrain was her husband, King Henry II. Another soothsayer had predicted that Henry should avoid close combat around his 41st year or he might die from a blow to the head.

The queen summoned Nostradamus to Paris in 1556 to explain the quatrain. While there, he was ordered to create astrological charts for Catherine's seven children. Nostradamus saw tragedy awaiting all of the royal family. He prophesied that four sons would become kings, but all of their reigns would end in tragedy. Rather than tell Catherine the truth and risk her wrath, he said simply all her sons would be kings. His prediction was close. Although only three sons rose to the throne, their reigns all ended badly.

Meanwhile, Henry had no interest in the tales of soothsayers, which proved a fatal mistake. Three years after Nostradamus visited, Henry, then 41 years old, engaged in several jousting competitions with other nobles on the day of his daughter's wedding. The object of jousting is to knock a rival off his horse with a blunt wooden lance. Late in the day Henry faced off against Gabriel de Lorges of the Scottish guard, who used a lion as an emblem. The two men charged each other, and de Lorges's lance hit Henry in the chest and snapped. The sharp, broken end pierced the king's gold-embossed helmet, the "golden cage." These "two wounds in one" put out Henry's eye and drove the severed lance into his brain. The king did not die immediately but died "a cruel death" screaming in agony for 10 days before a gangrene infection finally killed him.

Skeptics have pointed out that a jousting tournament is not a "field of combat" and that Henry's opponent was 35, hardly a "young lion." Despite these facts, Catherine believed the soothsayer's prophecies were startlingly accurate. The queen protected Nostradamus from officials who wanted to put him on trial for sorcery. However, mobs of religious peasants stoned Nostradamus's house in Salon, and he was forced to hide in the town jail for protection.

"Found Entirely Dead"

Nostradamus continued printing his yearly almanacs, and in the 1560s he was one of the most widely read authors in Europe. However, his health was deteriorating, and he could see his death on the horizon. In June 1566 he made out his will bequeathing a considerable sum of money, equal to about $300,000 today, to his wife and children. On the morning of July 2 his family, along with Chavigny, found Nostradamus dead on the floor between his bed and his workbench. Nearby, the last prophecy in his almanac,

dated for November 1567, was allegedly found. It stated:

> He will do no more; he will be gone to God:
> Close relatives, friends, brothers by blood,
> Found entirely dead near the bed and bench.[23]

Some believe Chavigny wrote this last prophecy as a fitting tribute to the famous soothsayer. Whether or not this is true, the perplexing quatrains by Nostradamus continued to echo for centuries after his death, and nearly every major catastrophe has been linked to the soothsayer's prophecies. This includes the Great London Fire in the seventeenth century, allegedly predicted in *Century 2*, quatrain 51:

> The blood of the just will commit a fault at London,
> Burnt through lightning of twenty threes and six;
> The ancient lady will fall from her high place,
> Several of the same sect will be killed.[24]

The great London fire began suddenly on September 2, 1666, the year "twenty threes and six." The fire destroyed most of London, the "ancient lady," and left 70,000 of the city's 80,000 residents homeless. Many people sought shelter in St. Paul's Cathedral, and several died when the church dome collapsed. "Several of the same sect" were killed.

The French Revolution

More than 100 years after the London Fire, Nostradamus is said to have predicted the bloody French Revolution, which began on July 14, 1789:

The black plague ravaged Europe at various times in history, leaving behind suffering and death (as depicted in this fifteenth-century Swiss manuscript illumination). When the plague again surfaced in Europe in the 1530s, Nostradamus put his medical training to work.

From the [enslaved] people, songs, chants and
requests,
While princes and lords captive in the prisons;
In the future headless idiots
Will be received as divine utterances.[25]

During the revolution, peasants or "the enslaved people" rose to power singing, chanting, and requesting their freedom. They imprisoned the king and other aristocrats, "princes and lords captive in the prisons," and chopped their heads off with a guillotine, making them "headless idiots."

Those who refuse to believe the prophetic powers of Nostradamus point out that his timeline is scrambled. The London fire is purportedly predicted in *Century 2* while the French Revolution, which came later, is prophesied in *Century 1*. Some historians believe Nostradamus was not predicting the French Revolution but making observations about the clear conflict between the lives of peasants and kings in his own time.

The Rise of Hitler

Believers say the prophecies of Nostradamus remain relevant in modern times. Some think the bloodiest, most horrific events of the past 100 years were described in *Centuries*. This is traced to Nostradamus's prophecies about a series of tyrannical leaders called Antichrists who would come to power. Some say that one of those Antichrists was French emperor Napoleon, who conquered most of Europe in the early nineteenth century. Another Antichrist was Nazi Adolf Hitler, who took control of Germany in 1932 and started World War II in 1939.

More than 100 million people died in World War II, and it is said Nostradamus predicted the horrific carnage in the sixteenth century. Quatrain 24 of *Century 2* seems to refer to Hitler as Hister: "The greater part of the region will be against the Hister . . . the German child will observe nothing."[26] A quatrain from *Century 9* is believed to prophesy Hitler's rise: "A captain of Great Germany will come to deliver through false help . . . his revolt will cause a great flow of blood."[27] Another reference to Hitler is allegedly found in *Century 10*:

> Stained with murder and enormous adulteries,
> The great enemy of the entire human race,
> Who will be worse than his forefathers, his uncles
> and his fathers
> Will be, in fire, battle and revolution, bloody and
> inhuman.[28]

Nostradamus made dozens of other prophecies purportedly linked to World War II, but skeptics point out that these predictions are not in chronological order. Some are from early chapters in *Centuries*, others come from prophecies written about later time periods. In addition, the word *Hister* is ancient Latin for the Danube River. Nonbelievers doubt Nostradamus was referring to Hitler. Nostradamus devotees counter that Hitler was born near the Danube, which makes the quatrain accurate.

One Thousand Years of Peace

By picking and choosing lines from the 942 prophecies written by Nostradamus, people claim he predicted just about every major event since his death. However, close inspection often calls the accuracy of the soothsayer's predictions into question. For example, books and websites quote *Century 9* quatrain 65 to claim Nostradamus predicted the 1969 Apollo moon landing: "He will come to take himself to the corner of Luna (the moon), where he will be taken and placed on alien land."[29] However, the rest of the quatrain states "The unripe fruits will be the subject of great scandal, Great blame, to one great praise."[30] No scandals were involved

with the moon landing, so believers often leave out the second part of the prophecy.

Nostradamus prophecies have been linked to the assassination of President John F. Kennedy in 1963, the US invasion of Iraq in 2003, and the destruction resulting from Hurricane Katrina, which devastated New Orleans in 2005. And there has been no shortage of speculation about Nostradamus's prophecies concerning the future. Most of the news is not good, however. *Centuries* is filled with predictions of plagues, famines, catastrophic battles, germ warfare, and the so-called third Antichrist who has not yet appeared. However, Hogue sees very positive news in prophecies from *Century 10*, which he believes covers the years 2026 to 3000: "The prophet predicts one thousand years of peace in which a galactic community becomes a reality and man enters a period where science and religion merge into a higher consciousness."[31]

Whatever the prospects for peace or war, Nostradamus makes one thing perfectly clear. The world will end in 3797. As Nostradamus describes the end of the world, "there will have fallen from the sky such a great abundance of fire, and of burning stones, that nothing will remain unconsumed . . . before the final conflagration."[32] Only time will tell if the world will end in fire more than 2230 years after the great soothsayer Nostradamus was found entirely dead. But until the world does end, people will doubtlessly quote the words of Nostradamus whenever calamity, catastrophe, and tragedy occur.

CHAPTER 4

Prophecies in the Modern Age

Every year after Christmas, soothsayers and psychics release predictions for the coming year. The prophecies are heard on radio and TV shows and printed in newspapers, magazines, and online columns. In December 2009 a clairvoyant known as Nikki, who is often heard on talk radio, predicted 2010 would see a worldwide power blackout, and a reptile invasion in El Paso. While these events did not take place, Nikki also predicted an oil spill in the Gulf of Mexico. This prediction came to pass and resulted in the worst environmental disaster in US history.

An online soothsayer called S. Sarich prophesied about celebrities. In one prediction for 2010, she put forth the bizarre prophecy that the ghost of pop singer Michael Jackson would materialize in the Vatican while Pope Benedict was giving a televised Easter address. This did not happen. St. Paul, Minnesota, psychic Fatima, who writes a newspaper column, did not risk predicting

unlikely events. She simply said "more health issues are on the way, there will be more wars . . . [and] we can expect 2010 to be more hectic than the past few years."[33] Few would disagree with Fatima's prophecies that people had issues with their health, engaged in war, or that 2010 was a frenzied year.

Whether predictions are accurate or odd, twenty-first-century prophesying mixes mystical guesswork with monetary gain. Psychic Nikki says she has many famous, and well-paying, clients, including Tom Cruise, Shirley MacLaine, Cher, Rod Stewart, and Matt Dillon. Oracle and author Sylvia Browne charges her clients up to $1,000 to hear predictions about their future. Following in the tradition of the Delphic oracles and Nostradamus, some modern psychics and soothsayers have turned their prophetic wisdom into profits.

The Sleeping Prophet

Not all soothsayers have used their powers to seek monetary gain. Edgar Cayce, one of the most influential prophesiers of the twentieth century, was famous but not rich. For 35 years, between 1910 and 1945, Cayce was the world's leading source of prophecy. Although his fame has faded in recent decades, the organization he founded, the Association for Research and Enlightenment (A.R.E.), continues to support Edgar Cayce Centers in 37 countries. These centers, with books and videos about prophecy, philosophy, and other occult matters, are visited by thousands of Cayce devotees every year.

Cayce, born in rural Kentucky in 1877, exhibited psychic abilities at an early age. Cayce was a terrible student, but when he was 10 years old he purportedly heard a voice that helped him improve his grades. A vision of a woman appeared in the middle of

Oil thickly coats the shore of an Alabama wildlife refuge in June 2010, just two months after the Deepwater Horizon spill in the Gulf of Mexico. The clairvoyant known as Nikki made many predictions for 2010—one of which was an oil spill in the gulf.

the night and told Cayce to sleep with his schoolbook under his pillow. He followed the instructions and awoke in the morning understanding its contents. Cayce claimed this gift stayed with him his entire life, and he often absorbed the content of books, "reading" them psychically as he slept.

Sounding Like a Doctor

Despite this ability to read while asleep, Cayce dropped out of school when he was 15. After a series of odd jobs, he became an insurance salesman when he was 23. However, in 1900 he contracted laryngitis that was so severe he could not talk for a year.

As a salesman who could not speak, Cayce was desperate for a cure. He visited an amateur hypnotist named Al Layne who put him into a deep hypnotic trance and told him to imagine a cure for his problem.

Although he seemed to be asleep, Cayce spoke forcefully. He diagnosed his problem saying his vocal cords were paralyzed due to nerve strain. This was caused by insufficient blood circulation in his voice box. Layne told him to cure the problem, and Cayce's throat purportedly turned bright red as he forced blood into his larynx. When he was brought out of the trance, Cayce could talk. Layne told him, "You know, you sounded just like a doctor when you were in your trance."[34]

The next day, the hypnotized Cayce performed a physical on Layne. He began speaking again like he had medical training, offering diagnoses, prescription drug recommendations, and health instructions. Layne was amazed and asked Cayce about his gift. Cayce said he was a clairvoyant, someone with the power to see what others cannot. Using his clairvoyance, Cayce could offer advice to the sick, view events taking place in distant locales, and see into the future.

The Sleeping Prophet

Within months of his hypnosis cure, Cayce learned to put himself into a trance. He began to treat patients from afar, offering medical help to those who called him on the phone or sent him letters. At first he took no money for his recommendations. However, this situation changed, and he began to charge a small fee after he gained national attention in 1910. A physician named Wesley Ketchum wrote an article about Cayce's miraculous ability to obtain psychic knowledge by tuning into the thoughts of others.

Ketchum stated that Cayce's mind "is in direct communication with all other subconscious minds, and is . . . gathering in this way all knowledge possessed by endless millions of other subconscious minds."[35]

After Ketchum's piece appeared in the *New York Times*, Cayce became famous overnight. Thousands of requests for medical help began pouring into Cayce's home. During the next decade, Cayce became one of the most famous healers in the world. He was known as the "sleeping prophet" because he provided his prophetic advice while lying down, seemingly asleep. In this state, Cayce gave readings by answering questions proposed by clients. After waking up from the trance, Cayce claimed to have no memory of his advice. In this era before audio recorders, the sleeping prophet's words were written down by a secretary.

Panic in the Money Centers

By 1922 Cayce claimed to have conducted more than 8,000 readings. Around this time he also developed a new talent. Cayce began performing what he called "life readings," entering a trance and visiting the past lives of his subjects. During these events, Cayce would claim to visit ancient Egypt, Greece, Babylonia, India, and China. By visiting the past, Cayce said he could help his clients understand the present and the future. He soon began prophesying about terrifying imminent events.

In March 1929 Cayce prophesied that the New York Stock Exchange on Wall Street would experience trouble. At the time, Cayce's fame had brought him into contact with several prominent businessmen. He told them to sell their entire stock portfolios. On April 6, 1929, Cayce once again warned, "There must surely come a break when there will be panic in the

money centers not only on Wall Street, but a closing of the banks in many centers."[36] The stock market crashed on October 29, 1929, confirming Cayce's prophecy. The Wall Street crash started the Great Depression, a worldwide economic catastrophe that lasted 10 years and resulted in thousands of bank failures throughout the world.

Cayce prophesied a bigger tragedy, scheduled to follow the Great Depression. In 1932 the sleeping prophet predicted that the world would turn to war in 1936. In 1935 Cayce said Germany and Austria would merge into a single country and Japan would join in this alliance. Three years later, Nazi soldiers marched into Austria and annexed the country as part of Germany. This was the first step toward World War II, in which Japan joined Germany to fight the United States, England, and other nations. In 1941 Cayce accurately predicted that World War II would end in 1945.

A New Order on Earth

Despite his often gloomy prophecies, Cayce made a prediction meant to give people hope during the depressing 1930s. In 1934 Cayce predicted that a savior of the human race, named John Penniel, would be born in 1936. Cayce predicted Penniel "would be beloved of all men in all places when the universality of God on the Earth has been proclaimed." However, Penniel, who would have been 74 in 2010, never "appeared as a messenger . . . [to] bring to earth a new order of things,"[37] as Cayce prophesied.

In the same reading Cayce predicted that by 1998 the "greater portion of Japan must go into the sea. The upper portion of Europe will be changed in the twinkling of an eye. . . . There will be upheaval in the Arctic and Antarctic . . . and there will be a shifting of the poles."[38] While the North and South Poles never

A long line forms in New York City in 1930, as hundreds who lost their jobs and savings seek help during the Great Depression. Shortly before the stock market crash of 1929, prophesier Edgar Cayce foretold of serious trouble in the banking industry and on Wall Street.

changed places in 1998, some believe the event will happen eventually. Devotees say the rest of the prediction was stunningly accurate. They believe Cayce predicted global warming, the melting of the polar ice caps, and the massive tsunami that destroyed much of northern Japan in 2011. This prediction was made decades before the science of global warming existed.

Whether his predictions were right or wrong, Cayce was a religious man who maintained a high moral standard. He was approached almost daily by businessmen and gamblers who wanted to get rich using his predictive powers. He turned these people down, preferring instead to focus on helping and healing humanity. In 1932 Cayce summed up his attitudes about fortune seekers while in a trance: "Man's answer to everything has been POWER—Power of money, Power of position, Power of wealth, Power of this, that or the other. This has NEVER been GOD'S way, will never be God's way."[39] This reading was one of 14,000 Cayce made before his death in 1945. The prophecies are now stored in a library at the Association for Research and Enlightenment in Virginia.

Death of a President

Countless Cayce fans can quote his accurate prophecies. However, many Cayce predictions were simply wrong. For example, he erroneously predicted that San Francisco and Los Angeles would be destroyed by Japanese bombers in World War II. Those who have studied prophecies and soothsayers have coined a term for the way people remember prophecies that come true and forget those that do not. It is called the "Jeane Dixon effect." It was named after a psychic who made one seemingly accurate prophecy and hundreds that never came true.

Dixon's most famous prediction came to her in 1952, when she was working in the real estate business. Dixon was praying before a candle in a church when she saw a vision of the White House. A blue-eyed, brown-haired man was standing before the building, and the number 1960 hovered in the air. A cloud appeared and, according to Dixon, spread from the number and "dripped down like chocolate frosting on a cake"[40] over the man. An inner voice told Dixon the man was an unnamed Democratic president who would die a violent death while in office. In 1956 Dixon's prediction appeared in *Parade* magazine.

Democrat John F. Kennedy, who had blue eyes and brown hair, was elected president in 1960. In June 1963 Kennedy was still alive and had only one more year to serve in his first term. When asked about the accuracy of her 1952 prophecy, Dixon reiterated: "I still see a large coffin being carried into the White House. This means that the President will meet death elsewhere and his body will be returned there for national mourning."[41] In the first weeks of November 1963, Dixon told three people that Kennedy was going to be shot. On November 22 her prophecy came true when Kennedy was gunned down in Dallas, Texas.

Wrong 99 Percent of the Time

After the president's death Dixon became a national celebrity. Every Christmas Dixon made predictions for the coming year that appeared in national magazines. Almost all of these prognostications were wrong. In the 1960s Dixon predicted the United States would engage in germ warfare with China and a monster comet would strike the Earth and cause millions of casualties. In the 1970s Dixon stated that the Roman Catholic Church would cease to exist and that the first female president would be elected in the United States by 1980. In the 1990s Dixon incorrectly predicted that talk show host Ellen DeGeneres would be arrested by the Secret Service when she crashed the presidential inauguration.

When Dixon died in 1997, her obituary in *USA Today* stated, "her prediction that President John F. Kennedy would die in office came true."[42] However, research shows Dixon predicted only that a Democrat would die in his first or second term, not necessarily Kennedy. And in 1960 she contradicted her 1952 prophecies, saying Kennedy's opponent, Richard M. Nixon would be elected president. And unlike her 1952 prophecy, the 1960 prediction was very specific: "John F. Kennedy would fail to win the presidency."[43]

Prophetic Maya Calendars

The Maya system of calendar prophecy was incredibly complicated because they used four separate calendars interlocked with one another. The Sacred Round calendar has 20 named days combined with a number between 1 and 13, which makes it a 260-day calendar. The days are named after a variety of things including Dog, Monkey, Yellow, Thought, Lefthanded, Thunder, and Death. This means a particular day on the Sacred Round might be Monkey the 13. Soothsayers used the Sacred Round as a tool to provide birth horoscopes for babies.

Despite her spotty record, Dixon advised politicians and presidents. Although Nixon lost in 1960 he was elected eight years later. And Nixon must have believed in Dixon's powers. In 1972 he set up a cabinet committee on counterterrorism after Dixon predicted a terrorist attack in the United States. Like 99 percent of Dixon's other predictions, this did not happen as predicted.

A second Maya calendar is called Vague Year. With 365 days it closely resembles the modern calendar. The Vague Year is composed of 18 20-day months and a short 5-day month. This was mostly used for practical purposes, to predict the best time for planting and harvesting crops.

The Maya created a method for linking the Sacred Round and the Vague Year calendars together to measure an even larger time cycle. Because of the mathematics involved, the combination of the 260- and 365-day cycles results in what is called a Calendar Round of 18,980 days—about 52 years. The Maya believed that the final days of each 52-year cycle in the Calendar Round would be marred by strife, calamity, and bad luck. The gods would observe how the Maya dealt with these problems and decide whether to grant the people another 52-year cycle.

Modern Prophecies and the Ancient Maya

Dixon made predictions about the immediate future that were bound to be proved or disproved in her lifetime. But in recent years one prophecy—made a very long time ago—has received a great deal of attention. The ancient Maya people, who lived in present-day Belize, El Salvador, Guatemala, and southern

Mexico, invented a complex series of calendars thousands of years ago. These calendars were used to make predictions for centuries into the future. But the last date on the sacred Long Count calendar is December 21, 2012. The prophetic significance of this date is not mentioned in any ancient Maya texts. But in the 1990s the year 2012 became a focus of fascination for soothsayers, prophets, and disaster devotees throughout the world.

The concept of a 2012 apocalypse has spawned countless books, articles, websites, TV shows, hit songs, and even a blockbuster Hollywood disaster film. All this speculation is based on an incredibly complicated calendar system invented more than 2,000 years ago.

Maya civilization flourished deep in the jungles of Central America between approximately 400 BC and AD 900. The Maya built pyramids, royal palaces, and monuments covered with intricate picture writing called hieroglyphics. Much of this writing is concerned with prophecy and magic that is based on the movements of the sun, moon, planets, and stars.

Using only the naked eye, Maya priests, mathematicians, and astronomers devised one of the most highly developed astronomy systems of any people anywhere in the world at the time. These intricate systems served religious purposes. The Maya believed that time, numbers, and the movement of the planets were ruled by gods. By keeping extremely accurate records on calendars, Maya rulers believed that they could communicate with the gods, understand and evaluate events around them, and even gaze into the future. Archaeologist Eric Thompson explains that the Mayas' "skill with numbers developed because accurate calculations were important to divination. They developed astronomical observation to support astrology—a basic element in their religious beliefs."[44]

The Long Count Calendar

The Maya calendar system is incredibly complicated, developed by priests and soothsayers for two reasons, to measure time and to prophesy. Each day and number on the ancient Maya calendar is associated with a specific deity, a god or goddess that holds direct influence over that day. In the large pantheon of Maya deities, these divine beings can be helpful, malevolent, or a combination of good and evil. Maya soothsayers were skilled at prophesying the future based on the deities and heavenly omens associated with each day.

The Maya had several different calendars for various purposes. One, called the Sacred Year, was used mainly to create horoscopes. A second, the Vague Year calendar, provided agricultural predictions. And a linking of the two, called the Sacred Round, provided soothsayers with information about good and bad omens for each day in the future. The calendar that attracted the most attention in the twenty-first century is called the Long Count calendar. This was invented using astronomical observations made over a period of several hundred years in the third and fourth centuries BC. As a result of this protracted effort, the Long Count calendar tracks time for a period of 5,125 years.

Every 5,125 year period on the Long Count calendar is called a great creation cycle. The cycles are discussed in the Maya creation story called the *Popul Vuh.* Like the calendar that tracks the tale, the *Popul Vuh* is an amazingly complex story that describes four creation cycles. The first cycle began when the gods tried to create humans from mud, wood, and rushes but failed. During the second creation cycle two divine boys known as the Hero Twins defeated the lords of the Underworld in a ball game that resembles modern-day soccer. After their victory over death, the

Hero Twins rose to the sky as the sun and Venus. During the third creation cycle, the Maya people were successfully created from corn. The fourth creation cycle began as Maya society spread throughout Central America. Archaeologists who have studied the dates in ancient Maya writings determined that the fourth great creation cycle started on August 11, 3114 BC. December 21, 2012, marks the end of this 5,125-year cycle, according to the Long Count calendar.

This beginning of the fifth cycle is at the center of the modern 2012 phenomenon, sometimes called 2012ology or twenty-twelveology. This is a belief that something of consequence will take place during the beginning of the fifth cycle. Some say fifth-cycle events will lead to the destruction of the planet.

"Fed Up with This Stuff"

A great debate continues as to what the Maya expected to happen at the beginning of the fifth creation cycle. Most Maya scholars believe that the date was only meant to mark the end of one 5,125-year cycle and the beginning of another. As Maya archaeologist José Huchim explained in 2010, "In the way of Mayan thinking, it's only a cyclical period which comes to an end. The Mayans never imagined it as a catastrophic date."[45] Huchim also points out that Maya inscriptions that predict the future consistently show that they expected life to go on pretty much the same forever. In the ancient town of Palenque, for example, they predicted that people in the year AD 4772 would be celebrating the anniversary of the coronation of their great king Pakal. Archaeologists also explain that the ancient Maya did not believe in the concept of apocalypse or Armageddon. These terms are used in the Bible, a book that was not introduced to the

The ancient Maya had many skilled soothsayers, whose prophecies were based on the gods and heavenly omens. Their various calendars (one of which is pictured) guided their daily activities but did not, as some believe, actually foretell the world's end in 2012.

people of this region until the sixteenth century AD.

Millions of Maya continue to live in their ancestral homelands, and few believe in 2012ology. Maya elder Apolinario Chile Pixtun commented that when he traveled in 2009 he was bombarded with frantic questions about the end of the world. "I came back from England last year and, man, they had me fed up with this stuff."[46] Whatever Maya people felt about the phenomenon, 2012 hysteria

The last day on
the Maya Long
Count calendar is
December 21, 2012.

spread throughout the Western world in the second half of the 2000s. Some people were very frightened. According to Cornell University astronomer Ann Martin, "We're getting e-mails from fourth-graders who are saying that they're too young to die. We had a mother of two young children who was afraid she wouldn't live to see them grow up."[47]

Since the Maya made no specific predictions about the end of the fourth cycle, 2012ologists were free to invent prophecies. The event was associated with the destruction of the Earth through global warming. Some echoed Cayce, prophesying a shift in the North and South Poles which would flip the planet upside down.

Many 2012ologists seem to be worried about the Earth colliding with a planet called Nibiru. In June 2009 the US space agency NASA stated that it had received over 1,000 questions about Nibiru. Correspondents feared Nibiru was going to pass so close to Earth that catastrophic earthquakes, superhot volcanic eruptions, and deadly tidal waves would result. NASA had to set up a web page to educate people that no such planet as Nibiru exists. The story was a hoax spread by viral e-mails on the Internet, a phenomenon that also mentioned an alien invasion was prophesied for 2012.

Wrong Date?

Not all 2012ologists promote doomsday scenarios. Some have predicted the fifth great cycle will usher in a new era of peace and love. Beyond the positive or negative implications are claims that the great cycles were calculated incorrectly. This mistake is a result of the complexities of interpreting complicated Maya calendars written in hieroglyphs. Some say the fourth cycle actually began on 3189 BC, not on 3114. That would mean the fifth cycle begins in AD 2087.

Cynical observers believe that 2012ology is simply a way for some to make money from the fears and ignorance of the general public. More than 200 books have been published about 2012ology. Meanwhile, thousands of website soothsayers offer readings and consultations about what the phenomenon means.

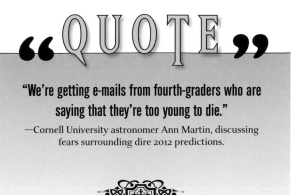

Sandra Noble, executive director of the Foundation for the Advancement of Mesoamerican Studies, which provides educational resources about the Maya, comments on the growth of the 2012 industry: "For the ancient Maya, it was a huge celebration to make it to the end of a whole cycle. [To call it a doomsday] is a complete fabrication and a chance for a lot of people to cash in."[48]

Like thousands of other predictions made in recent decades, ancient Maya prophecies have been used to create hope, fear, and monetary profit. Most of the prophecies are dead wrong. But the future continues to fascinate high-tech travelers in the twenty-first century much as it did the ancient Maya staring at the night sky with wonder thousands of years ago.

CHAPTER 5

Failed Prophecies

In the late 1990s the predictions were dire, and the media blared the bad news: Millions of computers manufactured in the 1980s and 1990s would fail on January 1, 2000. The computers included those that ran air traffic control systems, nuclear power plants, banks, and countless other vital systems on which civilization had become dependent. The millennium bug, simply called Y2K for Year 2000, was a result of computer programmers using only two digits to indicate the year. This was not a problem during the years such as 1987, 1990, or 1999. But when the clock rolled over to "00," it was feared the computers would not understand the date, reading it as 1900 or 199900. This would cause the computers to crash.

As the clock ticked toward midnight on December 31, 1999, governments and corporations spent over $300 billion to make sure their computers would function in the new year. Computer programmers throughout the world worked around the clock to prevent disastrous computer crashes. But software engineers were not the only ones working overtime. Those who profited from fears of the future were generating countless print ads, e-mails, and commercials filled with doomsday prophecies. There were dire predictions that planes would fall out of the sky, food, gas, and other necessities would become unavailable, and banks would fail. This would usher in a worldwide economic disaster followed by violent riots and eventual mass starvation.

In December 1999, gun sales increased, stores sold out of canned food and toilet paper, and people emptied their bank accounts to have cash on hand. On December 27 the politically powerful televangelist the Reverend Jerry Falwell addressed his followers: "Y2K is God's instrument to shake this nation, to humble this nation . . . to confound our language, to jam our communications, scatter our efforts, and judge us for our sin and rebellion for going against his lordship."[49]

"A Prophetic Word"

Falwell was not the only well-known preacher prophesying about Y2K. On the Trinity Broadcasting Network (TBN), evangelist Benny Hinn spoke often about Y2K fears. Hinn was a best-selling author and host of the TV program *This Is Your Day*. On his show, Hinn practiced faith healing, purportedly curing people of cancer, AIDS, and other diseases through prayer.

Hinn warned his TV audience that 1999 had been a year of plenty but that 2000 would bring disaster. Although Hinn's TV ministry raised over $50 million a year in the 1990s, he told his audience that those who did not increase their contributions to his church would not survive the year 2000. Even those who had

In the 990s
Europeans
experienced
End Times hysteria
when Halley's comet
streaked across
the sky and Mount
Vesuvius erupted
in Italy.

already donated were ordered to call back and double their donations or face disaster. Hinn put forth his prophetic message, speaking directly into the TV camera:

> The Lord has said to me that this year, 1999, would be the greatest year for the body of Christ, economically and spiritually, but beginning in the year 2000, disasters would hit in the world, economically and otherwise, and only those in the church who have been giving to God would be spared. So when I say to you here and in your home, increase your seed [monetary donation], God knows you can and you must because if you do not, you will be the one to suffer. . . . I'm giving you a prophetic word. . . . I'm telling you tonight, I'm speaking prophetically. Obey the Lord![50]

Catastrophic disasters did not hit the world in 2000. Most of Hinn's followers, even those that did not donate, did not suffer the Lord's punishment. Despite his failed prophecy Hinn continued to raise tens of millions of dollars throughout the following decade. In 2011 *This Is Your Day* was one of the most popular Christian TV programs in the world.

Various Torments

Hinn was certainly not the first religious doomsayer to make inaccurate prophecies concerning a new millennium. In AD 1000, many Christians anticipated the Apocalypse, as stated in the prophecies of Revelation. This was based on the belief that the new millennium arrived exactly 1,000 years after the first coming of Jesus. The dire predictions of a final battle of Armageddon began around the 950s. They did not stop until after 1033, which was 1,000 years after the death of Jesus.

In 950, a French abbot named Adso of Montier-en-Der was among the first to associate doomsday prophecies with the millennium. These were spelled out in a letter he wrote to the French king called "Treatise on the Antichrist." Adso predicted that the "Antichrist, the devil's son and the worst master of evil . . . will plague the whole world with great persecution and torture the whole people of God with various torments for three and a half years."[51] Copies of Adso's letter were widely circulated among the clergy of Europe. In the following years, fears of the End Times Apocalypse were stoked in thousands of churches every Sunday.

As the first millennium approached, anxiety gripped the populace. Almost every major event was seen as a sign that the prophecies of Revelation had begun. A solar eclipse in 968 created widespread panic in Germany. In France the death of King Louis V in 987 was viewed as an omen of Armageddon. Two years later, Halley's comet streaked across the sky, increasing fears that the Day of Judgment was at hand. In 991 and 999 two major eruptions of Mount Vesuvius in Italy added to millennial apocalypse panic.

During the late 990s waves of non-Christians converted to Catholicism. In France and Italy hundreds of older churches were rebuilt or refurbished. In December 999 the End Times hysteria reached fever pitch. Christians gathered in open fields to pray beneath crucifixes. Some gave away their worldly goods to the poor to purify themselves.

Hundreds of people abandoned their farms and villages to

When Halley's comet (pictured) streaked across the sky shortly before the year 1000, fears spread throughout Europe that the Day of Judgment was at hand. Other major events were also seen as a sign that the prophecies in Revelation had begun.

make pilgrimages to Jerusalem. Millennium researcher Richard Landes describes the scene: "Never before had so large and illustrious a contingent of Christian faithful, lay and clerical, set out on the greatest and most arduous of all the pilgrimages. They would take the land route, through the wilds of Hungary only recently converted, through Constantinople, through Moslem-held Syria and Palestine."[52] When the year turned to 1000, nothing happened, and normal daily life resumed. However, the prophets of doom never stopped predicting the end of the world. In the seventeenth century, the year 1666 stirred fears, since it was a combination of the millennium (1000) and the Mark of the Beast (666) in Revelation. While most of London burned to the ground in 1666, a worldwide apocalypse was avoided.

An Apocalyptic Cleansing

Most predictions of doom in earlier times had limited impact. However, in the nineteenth century a few prophets of apocalypse were able to attract large numbers of followers and form End Times sects. The first such mass movement was founded by a New York farmer and Baptist minister named William Miller. In the early 1820s Miller perused the Old Testament searching for an exact date of the Second Coming. He thought he found his answer in Daniel 8:14: "And [God] said unto me, Unto two thousand and three hundred days; then shall the sanctuary be cleansed."

Miller decided this verse meant that when God spoke of cleansing a sanctuary, he meant purifying the entire Earth. According to Miller's calculations, the cleansing would happen not in 2,300 days, but in 2,300 years. Miller then concluded that the prophecy was made in 457 BC on the first day of the Jewish new year, a holiday called Rosh Hashanah. Miller did some math and determined an apocalyptic cleansing of the Earth would take place sometime in the Jewish new year between 1843 and 1844. Sinners would be sent to hell, while believers were destined for heavenly glory.

The Time of the End

Miller began preaching in 1831. In 1832 he published a series of 16 articles about his End Times theory in a Vermont Baptist newspaper. The articles brought Miller extensive attention. He was suddenly deluged with letters from people wishing to hear his theories about the end of the world. He was invited to preach in so many churches he found it impossible to honor all the requests. To publicize his views Miller published a short, 64-page tract called *Evidence from Scripture and History of the Second*

Coming of Christ, About the Year 1844: Exhibited in a Course of Lectures.

By 1840 Miller had attracted about 100,000 devotees known as the Millerites. At this time about 1 out of every 100 American citizens was a member of this group. Millerites were convinced the end was near and passed a resolution at an 1842 convention: "Resolved: that in the opinion of this conference, there are most serious and important reasons for believing that God has revealed the time of the end of the world, and that the time is 1843."[53]

As the day of reckoning drew near, thousands of Millerites prepared for the impending return of Jesus Christ. They forgave debts, sold their worldly goods, and gave away their money to charities. However, 1843 came and went without God cleansing the Earth from sin. Millerites took comfort in the fact that they technically had until mid-1844 for their beliefs to come true.

In February 1844 Miller spoke to 5,000 followers in Philadelphia. He predicted that Jesus would appear within one month, around March 18 or 19. There was widespread disappointment when Jesus did not arrive as predicted. New calculations were made, and a Millerite preacher named Samuel Snow prophesied another date. Snow said the end of the world would arrive in little more than seven months. This became known as the "seven-months message" and the "true midnight cry,"[54] and it quickly spread throughout New England.

The Great Disappointment

On October 22 thousands of Millerites gathered in small groups waiting for the end. Snow was from Exeter, New Hampshire, and this became the site of the largest Millerite gathering. Thousands assembled on a hilltop as the sun set, certain that the prophecy was correct. They wept, sang, and hugged their families and friends. Some were overwhelmed by feelings of cosmic glory, according to researcher Clifford A. Pickover: "Millerites actually attempted to fly bodily to heaven. Some followers donned wings, climbed trees, and prayed to the lord to lift them up. Inevitably several devout followers broke their arms when they jumped from the trees."[55]

As midnight came and went, Jesus did not appear in the heavens. When nothing happened, many Millerites were left sad and bitter. Newspapers of the day called this event the Great Disappointment. However, about 500 Millerites kept their faith and continued to study the Bible for signs of the Second Coming. Miller died in 1849 and was convinced until the end that his prophecies were correct, even if the dates were wrong.

The Advent

Miller was not the only person who continued to believe that the second coming and the battle of Armageddon were on the horizon. His teachings likely influenced Joseph Smith Jr., founder of the Mormon church. In 1835 Smith said that a voice from heaven told him, "If thou livest until thou art eighty-five years old [until December 1890], thou shalt see the face of the Son of Man [Jesus]."[56] Smith never had a chance to prove his prophecy. He died after being attacked by a mob in 1844.

Smith was not a Millerite, but several Miller devotees formed their own religions after the Great Disappointment. Jonas Wendell founded the religious movement called Adventism, which refers to the belief that the Second Advent, or Second Coming, of Jesus is imminent. Early Adventists were Millerites who believed that Jesus had arrived on October 22, as prophesied by

The End of the World as We Know It

In 1987 the rock band R.E.M. had their first hit with the song "It's the End of the World as We Know It (And I Feel Fine)." In the twenty-first century, survivalists use the word TEOTWAWKI, an acronym of "The End Of The World As We Know It," to describe what they believe is a certain apocalypse within their lifetimes.

The TEOTWAWKI movement is fueled by prophecies mentioned in Revelation. The most common doomsday scenarios include a massive volcanic erup-

Miller. However, he did not appear as a physical being but instead arrived invisibly in a spiritual form. Several spiritual groups grew out of the Adventist movement, including the Seventh-Day Adventist Church.

The Jehovah's Witnesses denomination can also trace its roots

tion, earthquakes, a worldwide pandemic, or a large asteroid striking the Earth. One TEOTWAWKI website advises survivalists to watch for the appearance of the Four Horsemen of the Apocalypse in coming years. More modern fears include nuclear strikes on US cities, chemical spills, a cutoff of the world oil supply, or a massive terrorist attack. Whatever the case, TEOTWAW-KI events are expected to cause a total breakdown in civilization when money becomes worthless and food, fuel, water, and electricity supplies are interrupted. Hundreds of doomsday prophecies are on the Internet, many put forth by people hoping to profit from fears of the End Times. TEOTWAWKI websites sell survivalist books, freeze-dried food, weapons, tools, and camping equipment to those waiting for the Second Coming.

back to the Millerites. In 1870 an 18-year-old from Pittsburgh named Charles Taze Russell attended an Adventist service given by Wendell. Russell, who went on to found the Jehovah's Witnesses, heard Wendell prophesy that the Second Coming would occur four years hence, in 1874. During the next several years,

Russell became intensely interested in the writings of Millerite ministers.

Wendell's prediction of Armageddon in 1874 proved to be in error, so Russell picked a new date, April 1878, for the Second Coming. In preparation, he sold the five successful clothing stores owned by his family for a sum equal to $7 million today. He spent the money on a publishing company to print books and pamphlets announcing the end of the world.

Russell was undeterred when April 1878 did not usher in a new age. Within a year, he began publishing the journal *Zion's Watch Tower* (later shortened to *Watch Tower*). In 1881 Russell formed the Zion's Watch Tower Bible and Tract Society to offer free public lectures and to publish and distribute Bibles, books, papers, pamphlets, and other Bible literature.

Russell's publishing business was profitable, and he used his journals to promote his prophecies about the end of the world. In 1889 he wrote that the battle between good and evil had already begun and that Armageddon would occur on October 1, 1914. According to Russell, at that time all politicians, kings, and other secular rulers would be overthrown so God's kingdom could be established on Earth.

World War I started on July 28, 1914, and this calamitous war resulted in the death of millions. However, when Armageddon did not commence on October 1, Russell justified his failed prophecy while sounding much like the Millerites of the nineteenth century. He claimed the Lord had returned, but invisibly.

When Russell died in 1916, he was writing weekly religious columns followed by 15 million readers. Russell's successor, Joseph Rutherford, took over the Watch Tower Bible and Tract Society, and the group continued to publish End Time prophecies, choosing the years 1918, 1920, and 1925 for the end of the world. The Watch Tower group, which changed its name to Jehovah's Witnesses in 1931, carried on, and its predictions of Armageddon continued.

A Happy Beginning

One failed prophecy almost spelled the end, not of time, but of the Jehovah's Witnesses. *Watch Tower* magazine often made the assertion that God proclaimed his will only through the Jehovah's Witnesses organization, the prophecies of which were absolutely true and could not be doubted. In 1966 *Watch Tower* began publishing prophecies stating that 1975 would be the year when all sinners were to die while the righteous ascended to heaven. This prophecy, like Miller's, was based on math. *Watch Tower* put forth the proposition that God created the first man, Adam, in 4026 BC. According to the magazine's calculations, the year 1975 would be the 6,000th anniversary of this miracle.

Writers in *Watch Tower* encouraged Jehovah's Witnesses to sell their homes, quit their jobs, and not make any plans after 1975. Members were also encouraged to go door-to-door preaching the End Times message. However, when 1976 arrived without the predicted apocalypse, church membership plunged, and the Jehovah's Witnesses movement almost ceased to exist. The movement eventually attracted new followers, and since 1976 *Watch Tower* has been more careful about publishing prophecies about the Great Tribulation predicted in Revelation.

Despite other failed prophecies, Jehovah's Witnesses continue to maintain that Jesus did arrive invisibly in 1914 and that End Times events began at that time. The signs of apocalypse continue and include ongoing wars throughout the world, earthquakes, tsunamis, deadly diseases such as AIDS, and fears of global warming

"Some followers donned wings, climbed trees, and prayed to the lord to lift them up. Inevitably several devout followers broke their arms when they jumped from the trees."

—Researcher Clifford A. Pickover discussing nineteenth-century Millerites waiting for the apocalypse.

and nuclear war. However, according to the *Watch Tower* website, there is no reason to fear:

"Armageddon . . . provides a basis for hope. The war of Armageddon will cleanse the earth of all corruption and wickedness and open the way for a righteous new system of things. . . . Instead of being a frightening cataclysmic end, Armageddon will signal a happy beginning for righteous individuals, who will live forever on a paradise earth."[57]

Church Universal and Triumphant

Most predictions about the end of the world come from Christian groups. However, in the 1980s a New Age organization called the Church Universal and Triumphant made headlines with a dire prophecy.

The roots of the Church Universal and Triumphant can be traced to 1958 when Mark Prophet founded the Summit Lighthouse. He was later joined by his wife, Elizabeth Clare Prophet, also known as Guru Ma. Mark and Elizabeth Prophet claimed that members of the Summit Lighthouse organization were superior beings, called Ascended Masters. The Ascended Masters began as human beings but became immortal through spiritual enlightenment, meditation, and other religious practices that originated in India. According to Elizabeth Clare Prophet, the Ascended Masters are related to the prophets mentioned in the Bible.

Mark Prophet died of a stroke in 1973, but the night before his death he told Elizabeth to plan for the end of civilization by learning survivalist techniques. Survivalists believe the end is near and plan for a breakdown of modern society. To survive after the Apocalypse, they build up supplies of food and water, take first aid courses, and collect arms for self-defense.

In 1975 Prophet established the Church Universal and Triumphant (CUT) in Southern California. The teachings of the church were derived from messages supposedly transmitted by Ascended Masters, Buddha, Jesus, and a mysterious being Prophet called the "head of the Cosmic Secret Service."[58] She offered survivalist courses for adherents, and CUT membership grew to about 50,000.

"It's Not Over"

In 1988 Prophet announced a nuclear missile strike would destroy the United States on April 23, 1990. In order to survive, the church spent $20 million to build 40 underground bomb shelters on a 12,000-acre ranch (4,856ha) in Corwin Springs, Montana, near Yellowstone National Park. About 700 members moved into the shelters, which were 20 feet (6m) underground and protected by heavy steel doors. The bombproof rooms were filled with crates of dried fish, canned meat, cooking oil, and dozens of books written by the Prophets. While preparing for doom, members of the Church Universal and Triumphant attracted the attention of federal authorities when they began stockpiling assault rifles and bought several armored personnel carriers as part of what Prophet called a post–nuclear war reemergence plan.

In March 1990 thousands of CUT members traveled to the Yellowstone area to enter the bomb shelters and wait for the end. When the bombs did not fall, Prophet claimed the entire exercise was a drill. In the aftermath, church membership dwindled to about 10,000 adherents.

After the predictions of doom went unrealized, church members gave up their firearms in exchange for land under an agreement with federal authorities. Prophet was stricken with Alzheimer's disease in 1999 and died in 2009. As her charismatic presence faded, most of her followers left or moved into the nearby towns of Livingston and Bozeman. In 2011 several hundred members were keeping the Church Universal and Triumphant alive, surviving on money collected from the sales of CDs and books filled with Prophet's teachings.

Observers estimate that fewer than 1,000 CUT members remain worldwide. Church leaders refuse to give a number, saying membership information is proprietary. Church members continue to preach that global financial problems, terrorism, and the wars in Iraq and Afghanistan suggest that doomsday is coming soon. As Lois Drake, the church's copresident, says, "What we believe is that [the apocalypse] has been happening for a number of years. It's not over." They maintain the bomb shelters as "an insurance policy."[59]

"Rash Conjectures of Fanciful Men"

The doomsday prophecies of Elizabeth Clare Prophet, William Miller, and Benny Hinn would not have surprised famed seventeenth-century scientist Isaac Newton. While Newton is remembered as a mathematician and physicist who discovered the concept of gravity, a lesser-known fact is that he was deeply religious. Newton claimed he was specially chosen by God to interpret biblical prophecy.

In 2003 the media reported that Newton wrote a previously unpublished paper in 1705 that predicted the end of the world. However, he noted in the prediction that he had a strong distaste for self-appointed prophesiers. Despite this disclaimer, Newton

went on to choose the year 2060 as a final date for humanity's existence on Earth: "[The world] may end later, but I see no reason for it ending sooner. This I mention not to assert when the time of the end shall be, but to put a stop to the rash conjectures of fanciful men who are frequently predicting the time of the end, and by doing so bring the sacred prophecies into discredit as often as their predictions fail."[60]

Newton clearly made his prediction to quiet false prophets who made a mockery of the prophecies in the Bible. But whatever his motivation, Newton will likely be proved wrong about 2060. And it is certain that in the late 2050s, thousands of "soothsayers" will begin predicting imminent catastrophe based on Newton's writings.

Whether or not Newton is right, some things are certain. Just as death will come to all, every society and culture—no matter how powerful—will someday cease to exist. And eventually, the world will end when the sun burns out billions of years in the future. Before that time, the when, how, and why of doomsday remains a matter of speculation. For those who live without fear of apocalypse, the future can be faced with joy and hope instead of dread.

NOTES

Introduction: Practicing the Art of Prophecy

1. Quoted in Michael R. Best and Frank H. Brightman, eds., *The Book of Secrets of Albertus Magnus of the Virtues of Herbs, Stones, and Certain Beasts; Also a Book of the Marvels of the World*. York Beach, ME: Red Wheel/Weiser, p. 98.

Chapter 1: Peering into the Future

2. Quoted in Peter V. Jones and Keith C. Sidwell, *The World of Rome: An Introduction to Roman Culture*. Cambridge: Cambridge University Press, 2003, p. 250.
3. Pausanias, "Description of Greece, Book I: Attica," Internet Ancient History Sourcebook, Fordham University, 1998. www.fordham.edu/halsall.
4. Philipp Vandenberg, *The Mystery of the Oracles*. New York: Macmillan, 1982, p. 229.
5. Pausanias, "Description of Greece, Book I: Attica."
6. Quoted in Justine Glass, *They Foresaw the Future*. New York: G.P. Putnam's

Sons, 1969, p. 42.
7. Quoted in Vandenberg, *The Mystery of the Oracles*, pp. 195–96.
8. Quoted in Paul Halsall, "The Internet Ancient History Sourcebook: The Reports of the Magicians & Astrologers of Nineveh & Babylon, c. 2500–670 BCE," Fordham University, March 1999, www.fordham.edu/halsall.
9. Quoted in Peter Whitfield, *Astrology: A History*. New York: Harry N. Abrams, 2001, pp. 69–70.
10. Max Jacobi, "Astrology," Essan, October 4, 2010, www.essan.org.
11. Quoted in Nick Kollerstrom, "Galileo's Astrology," Skyscript, 2004. www.skyscript.co.uk.
12. Joan Quigley, "Protecting the President's Life," Global Oneness, 2010. www.experiencefestival.com.

Chapter 2: Prophecies and the Bible

13. Stephen F. Winward, *A Guide to the Prophets*. Richmond, VA: John Knox, 1969, p. 21.
14. Steven L. McKenzie, *How to Read the*

Bible. New York: Oxford University Press, 2005, p. 68.

15. Tom McIver, *The End of the World: An Annotated Bibliography.* Jefferson, NC: McFarland, 1999, p. 6.

Chapter 3: Nostradamus

16. Quoted in Love to Know, "Urban Legends Hoax," 2011. http://paranormal. lovetoknow.com.

17. Quoted in Edgar Leoni, *Nostradamus and His Prophecies.* New York: Bell, 1982, p. 309.

18. Quoted in Leoni, *Nostradamus and His Prophecies*, p. 17.

19. Quoted in Leoni, *Nostradamus and His Prophecies*, p. 19.

20. John Hogue, *Nostradamus & the Millennium.* Garden City, NY: Dolphin, 1987, p. 17.

21. Quoted in Leoni, *Nostradamus and His Prophecies*, p. 121.

22. Nostradamus, "Century I," Sacred Texts, 2010. www.sacred-texts.com.

23. Quoted in Leoni, *Nostradamus and His Prophecies*, p. 503.

24. Nostradamus, "Century II," Sacred Texts, 2010. www.sacred-texts.com.

25. Quoted in Leoni, *Nostradamus and His Prophecies*, p. 135.

26. Nostradamus, "Century II."

27. Quoted in Leoni, *Nostradamus and His Prophecies*, p. 409.

28. Quoted in Lee McCann, "Nostradamus, the Man Who Saw Through Time," Sacred Texts, 2010. www.sacred-texts.com.

29. Quoted in Hogue, *Nostradamus & the Millennium*, p. 95.

30. Quoted in Leoni, *Nostradamus and His Prophecies*, p. 401.

31. Hogue, *Nostradamus & The Millennium*, p. 205.

32. Quoted in Leoni, *Nostradamus and His Prophecies*, p. 129.

Chapter 4: Prophecies in the Modern Age

33. Quoted in Nora Leinen, "St. Paul Psychic Looks to 2010 and Beyond," *TC Daily Planet*, December 30, 2009. www.tc dailyplanet.net.

34. Quoted in Damon Wilson, *The Mammoth Book of Nostradamus and Other Prophets.* New York: Carroll & Graf, 2001, p. 356.

35. Quoted in Jess Stern, *Edgar Cayce: The Sleeping Prophet.* Garden City, NY: Doubleday, 1967, p. 6.

36. Quoted in Wilson, *The Mammoth Book of Nostradamus and Other Prophets*, p. 360.

37. Quoted in Wilson, *The Mammoth Book of Nostradamus and Other Prophets*, p. 361.

38. Quoted in Wilson, *The Mammoth Book of Nostradamus and Other Prophets*, p. 361.

39. Edgar Cayce, "Edgar Cayce on World Events," Edgar Cayce's A.R.E., 2011. www.edgarcayce.org.

40. Quoted in Ruth Montgomery, *A Gift of Prophecy: The Phenomenal Jeane Dixon.*

New York: William Morrow, 1965, p. 6.

41. Quoted in Montgomery, *A Gift of Prophecy*, p. 7.

42. Quoted in Cecil Adams, "Did Psychic Jeane Dixon Predict JFK's Assassination?" The Straight Dope, February 2, 2000. www.straightdope.com.

43. Quoted in Adams, "Did Psychic Jeane Dixon Predict JFK's Assassination?"

44. Quoted in Howard La Fay, "The Maya, Children of Time," *National Geographic*, December 1975, p. 738.

45. Quoted in *Independent* (London), "Experts to Explore Modern Mayan Version of '2012,'" February 20, 2010. www.independent.co.uk.

46. Quoted in *Sunday Telegraph* (London), "2012 Is Not the End of the World, Mayan Elder Insists," October 11, 2009. www.telegraph.co.uk.

47. Quoted in *Sunday Telegraph*, "2012 Is Not the End of the World, Mayan Elder Insists."

48. Quoted in Jeffrey MacDonald, "Does Maya Calendar Predict 2012 Apocalypse?" *USA Today*, March 27, 2007. www.usatoday.com.

Chapter 5: Failed Prophecies

49. Quoted in Hanna Rosin, "As Jan. 1 Draws Near, Doomsayers Reconsider," *Washington Post*, December 27, 1999.

50. Quoted in Teri Lee Earl, "(A Look Back) at Y2K Prophecies," Harvest NETwork, August 30, 2007. www.harvestnet.org.

51. Adso of Montier-en-Der, "Letters on the Origin and Time of the Antichrist," Apocalyptic Theories, October 30, 2000. www.apocalyptic-theories.com.

52. Richard Landes, "The Turbulent Career of a Monk of the Year 1000," Boston University, 1999. www.bu.edu.

53. Quoted in Clifford A. Pickover, *Dreaming of the Future*. Amherst, NY: Prometheus Books, 2001, p. 235.

54. George R. Knight, *Millennial Fever and the End of the World*. Boise: Pacific, 1993, p. 199.

55. Pickover, *Dreaming of the Future*, p. 235.

56. Quoted in J. Allan Danelek, *2012: Extinction or Utopia*. Woodbury, MN: Llewellyn, 2009, p. 39.

57. *Watch Tower*, "Armageddon: A Happy Ending," 2009. www.watchtower.org.

58. Quoted in "Keeper of Lighthouse Cult Cried Wolf Too Often," Rick A. Ross Institute, November 4, 2009. www.rickross.com.

59. Quoted in Mathew Brown, "Ready for Armageddon," Rick A. Ross Institute, November 24, 2008. www.rickross.com.

60. Quoted in Danelek, *2012*, p. 29.

FOR FURTHER RESEARCH

Books

J. Allan Danelek, *2012: Extinction or Utopia.* Woodbury, MN: Llewellyn, 2009.

Mark Heley, *101 Things You Should Know About 2012.* Avon, MA: Adams Media, 2011.

Doug Mauss, ed., *The Action Bible.* Colorado Springs, David C. Cook, 2010.

Shane Mountjoy, *The Maya.* New York: Chelsea House, 2011.

Robert M. Place, *Astrology and Divination.* New York: Checkmark, 2009.

Mario Reading, *Nostradamus: The Top 100 Prophecies.* Illustrated edition. New York: Watkins, 2010.

Websites

Edgar Cayce's A.R.E. (www.edgarcayce. org). The official site of Edgar Cayce's Association for Research and Enlightenment. Readers can find excerpts from Cayce's thousands of readings with essays linking the prophecies made in the last century to current events.

Failed End of the World Predictions (www.religioustolerance.org/end_wrl2.htm). A list of prophecies of doom from AD 30 to 1920 with links to detailed information concerning the facts and fallacies behind the predictions.

This site also contains extensive information about major religions, cults, nonconventional beliefs, and the 2012 end-of-the-world movements.

Internet Sacred Texts Archive (www.sacred-texts.com). The site has one of the largest collections of ancient books about traditional religion, spiritual practices, mythology, and folklore, including the Bible and the complete writings of Nostradamus.

Junior Skeptic (www.skeptic.com/junior_ skeptic). A site maintained by the Skeptics Society, Junior Skeptic provides facts and sheds light on classic paranormal beliefs like fortune-telling, prophecies, and soothsaying.

Nostradamus and Other Prophets, Prophecies, and Predictions (http:// hogueprophecy.com). Maintained by Nostradamus biographer John Hogue, this site contains extensive information about the sixteenth-century soothsayer as well as prophecies by the author concerning politics, global warming, and other current events.

Revelations 13.net (http://revelation13. net). This website links chapter 13 of the Book of Revelation with prophecies for the future, Nostradamus, and many unconventional ideas about disaster, doom, and destruction.

INDEX

Note: Boldface page numbers indicate illustrations.

A

K

Kennedy, John F., assassination of, 54, 62–63
Kepler, Johannes, 18
Ketchum, Wesley, 58–59

L

Landes, Richard, 76
Layne, Al, 58
life readings, 59
London, 1666 fire, 50, 52
Louis V (king of France), death of, 75

M

magicians, 6
Mark of the Beast, 30–31, 34, 37
Martin, Ann, 70
mathematics
    astrology and, 18–19
    to compute date of Apocalypse, 74–75, 77, 83
    Maya calendars and, 65, 66
Maya
    astronomy, 66
    calendars, 64–65, 66, 67–68, **69**
    civilization, 65–66
    2012ology, 68–71
McIver, Tom, 26
McKenzie, Steven L., 26
Medici family, 19, 48, 49
Middle Ages, 18
millennial prophecies, 72–76
millennium bug (Y2K) predictions, 72–73
Miller, William, 77–79
Millerites, 77–79, 81
moon landing, 53–54
Mormon church, 79
Morpheus, 10
Mount Vesuvius eruptions, 75

N

Nero (emperor of Rome), 31
New Age organizations, 84, 86–87
New Jerusalem, 36
New Testament. *See* Apocalypse, New Testament
        account
Newton, Isaac, 87–88
New York Stock Exchange, 59–60
New York Times (newspaper), 40
Nibiru, 70
Nikki, 55
Nixon, Richard M., 63, 64
Noble, Sandra, 71

Nostradamus, **44**
    biographical sketch of, 41–43
    death of, 49–50
    Pope Sixtus V and, 43
    popularity of, 8, 41
    on powers and use of prophecy, 46–47
    predictions of
        Apollo moon landing, 53–54
        end of world, 54
        French Revolution, 50–52
        Great London Fire, 50, 52
        Henry II, 47–48
        Hitler, 52–53
        Hurricane Katrina, 54
        Kennedy, 54
        own death, 49–50
        2001 attack on World Trade Center, 38–40
    process used by, 45
    writings of, 41, 45–48, 52–54
Nostredame, Michel de. *See* Nostradamus

O

Old Testament (Hebrew Bible)
    prophecies as warnings, 25–26
    prophecies of Ezekiel, 24–25, **27**
    prophecies of Zechariah, 28
    relationship of prophets to God, 23–24
onychomancy, 5
oracles
    Greek, 11–14, **17**
    sources of inspiration for, 6, 13
Oropos, Amphiareion of, 11–12

P

Pausanias, 11–12
Penniel, John, 60
Peretti, Felice (Pope Sixtus V), 43
Persia, 14
Pickover, Clifford A., 79
Pixtun, Apolinario Chile, 69
plagues
    in Book of Revelation, 34–35
    during Middle Ages, 41, 42–43, **51**
pope, associated with 666, 31
Popul Vuh (Maya creation story), 67–68
preterism theory, 36
profiting from prophecy
    Cayce and, 58, 61–62
    current psychics and soothsayers, 56
    Delphic oracles, 13
    Hinn, 73–74
    Nostradamus, 49
    2012ology, 71
Prophet, Elizabeth Clare, 84, 86–87

Prophet, Mark, 84
psychics, 6
pyromancers, 6
Pythia, 13, 14

Q

quatrains (of Nostradamus), 45, 47
Quigley, Joan, 16, 20–22

R

Reagan, Nancy, 20
Reagan, Ronald, 16, 20–22
R.E.M., 80
Revelation. *See* Apocalypse, New Testament
      account
Rome, ancient
    astrologers in, 16–18
    Caesar, 9–10, **11**
    Nero, 31
    Tiberius, 18
Rudolf II (emperor of Austria), 18
Russell, Charles Taze, 81–82
Rutherford, Joseph, 82

S

Sacred Round calendar, 64, 65, 67
Sacred Year calendar, 67
Sarich, S., 55
Satan
    as beast/Antichrist, 34
    as Dragon, 32
    final battle, 35
Scalinger, Julius-Cesar, 42, 43
scrying, 45
Second Coming, belief in
    by Adventists, 79–80
    by Jehovah's Witnesses, 81–84
    by Millerites, 77, 79, 81
    by survivalists, 81
seven seals, 29–31
Seventh-Day Adventist Church, 80
shamans, 6
666, significance in prophecy, 30–31, 34
skeptics
    arguments of, 8
    modern, 20–21
    of predictions of Nostradamus, 40, 53–54
sleeping prophet. *See* Cayce, Edgar
Smith, Joseph, Jr., 79
Snow, Samuel, 78
solar eclipse (968), 75
soothsayer, defined, 6–7

sorcery, 46
Spurinnia, 9–10
stars, reading. *See* astrology
Suetonius, 16–17
Summit Lighthouse, 84
survivalists, 80–81, 84, 86

T

Temple of Apollo at Delphi, 12–14, **17**
TEOTWAWKI movement, 80–81
Themistocles, 14
Theogenes, 16–18
This Is Your Day (television program), 73–74
Thompson, Eric, 66
Tiberius (emperor of Rome), 18
"Treatise on the Antichrist" (Adso of Montier-en-
      Dor), 75
Trinity Broadcasting Network (TBN), 73–74
truth, derivation of word, 6
"turn or burn" prophecies, 26
2012ology/twenty-twelveology, 68–71

V

Vague Year calendar, 65
Vandenberg, Philipp, 11–12
Vicar of the Son of God (papal title associated with
      666), 31

W

Watch Tower, 82, 83
Wendell, Jonas, 79–80, 81, 82
Winward, Stephen F., 24
Woe Trumpets, 32
World Trade Center, 2001 attack on, 38–40, **39**
World War II, 52–53, 60, 62

X

Xerxes, 14

Y

Y2K (computer millennium bug) predictions, 72–73

Z

Zechariah, prophecies of, 28
Zeus, 10
Zion's Watch Tower Bible and Tract Society, 82–83